Proclamation!

Proclamation!

A Christian Guide to Public Speaking

Blake J. Neff

Wipf & Stock
PUBLISHERS
Eugene, Oregon

PROCLAMATION!
A Christian Guide to Public Speaking

Copyright © 2007 Blake J. Neff. All rights reserved. Except for brief quotations in critical publications or reviews, no part of this book may be reproduced in any manner without prior written permission from the publisher. Write: Permissions, Wipf and Stock, 199 W. 8th Ave., Eugene, OR 97401.

Scripture taken from the *Holy Bible, New International Version*. Copyright 1973, 1978, 1984 by International Bible Society. Used by permission of Zondervan. All rights reserved.

All photographs are by Susan Ziegler and are reproduced by permission
Unless otherwise noted the persons and examples named in this book are hypothetical.

ISBN 13: 978-155635-094-8

Manufactured in the U.S.A.

Contents

Acknowledgments / vii

Chapter 1: Good Grief! Public Speaking / 1
Chapter 2: From the Other Side of the Lectern / 19
Chapter 3: Speak Confidently / 33
Chapter 4: Speak Ethically / 45
Chapter 5: Deciding on a Speech Topic / 59
Chapter 6: Developing the Speech / 77
Chapter 7: Designing the Speech / 101
Chapter 8: Delivering the Speech / 117
Chapter 9: Speeches to Inform / 133
Chapter 10: Speeches to Persuade / 149
Chapter 11: Speeches to Edify / 167
Chapter 12: Speeches to Celebrate / 181

Glossary / 195
Bibliography / 205

Acknowledgments

While the contents of this book including any errors and omissions are my own responsibility, I gratefully acknowledge the efforts of others who have helped to make the work possible. Bethany Brengan offered excellent editorial suggestions with a spirit of dedication and humility. Susan Ziegler, Indiana Wesleyan University photography student, produced the photographs in the midst of a busy academic schedule. Hundreds of public speaking students over the past two decades have not only helped to shape the text, but have tolerated the ranting of their instructor that no textbook was available adequately blending Christian faith with the best scholarship in the area of public speaking. With a prayer that at last such a book exists, I dedicate *Proclamation* to those former students.

1

Good Grief! Public Speaking

Chapter Challenges

A careful reading of Chapter 1 will provide insight into these chapter challenges:

1. What are the primary reasons to study public speaking?
2. Identify the five settings of communication.
3. What elements of communication are common to each of the five settings?

At the Student Union Roundtable

"Four great classes and public speaking." Janelle sighed as she looked over her schedule for the new semester.

"Yeah, bummer," agreed Cynthia. "Why is public speaking a general education requirement anyway? I'm nervous already, just thinking about having to stand up in front of the class to give a speech."

"At least you will be giving speeches in your mother-tongue," said Belsa with a grin. "If I could give speeches in Spanish, I'd look forward to the class. But in English, I'm not so sure."

"¡Oh sí, amigo!" Ryan laughed. "Your English is better than mine, even if you did just move to the States from Honduras a few months ago. Actually, I'm looking forward to public speaking. So we have to give a few speeches—that sure beats the one thousand pages of reading we've got in Old Testament Survey."

"Or the fifteen-page research paper in American History," said Jess with a sigh. "Besides, we've all agreed to meet here at the student union every day after chapel to study. How tough can it be?"

"I'm sure we can handle the things that we study for when we are together. But it's not the written work or the reading or the tests that I'm concerned about," Jannelle argued. "I'm just not excited about actually doing the public speaking, and I can't see any real value in it. What's the point?"

"I agree. Why do we have to take public speaking anyway?" Cynthia moaned as the others nodded their agreement.

Why Public Speaking?

This student union roundtable discussion is not unique. In fact, scenes like it are played out on campuses across America at the beginning of every new term. The question "Why must I take a course in public speaking?" is echoed again and again. Research indicates that the most common student-answer to the question is simply, "Because I have to."[1] But better reasons to take a course in public speaking exist than the fact that the best colleges and universities in America require it. Upon careful consideration, at least nine additional reasons to take a course in public speaking emerge.

---

1. Trank and Lewis, "Introductory Communication Course," 106–22.

Reason #1 Enhanced Interpersonal Relationships

In Genesis 2:18 God examined the work of creation and made the evaluative comment, "It is not good for the man to be alone" (New International Version). God then created a companion for Adam. Since that time human beings have been involved in interaction with others and in interpersonal relationships. Further, satisfaction in life depends to a large extent on an individual's ability to communicate within these relationships. Whether a person is among friends socially, at home with family members, interacting with coworkers on the job, or dialoging in a fellowship group at church, communication is an important key to life satisfaction.

Many aspects of general communication are explored in a public speaking class. The skills necessary to be effective at interpersonal communication are refined and honed even though the main focus is public address. For example, public speaking students learn to both improve their listening skills and sharpen their use of language. They also develop the ability to organize their thoughts and refine their ability to make use of various persuasive appeals. In short, successful public speaking students develop a more effective style of communication and hence improved interpersonal interactions and enhanced relationships.

Reason #2 Improved Academic Standing

The skills learned in a public speaking class are applicable in other academic pursuits. As a result, public speaking students often discover that, when they apply the techniques they have learned, they see marked improvement in their grades in other courses.

That was the case with Kevin, who waited until the second semester of his senior year to take the public speaking course required for his major. He had enrolled several times, but whenever he felt the symptoms of communication apprehension, he dropped the class. After successfully completing the course, Kevin lamented, "I should have stuck it out before. So many of the topics discussed would have helped me get better grades in all my other classes."

Kevin is absolutely right. For example, effective listening skills can be used to evaluate and absorb lectures in disciplines such as history, chemistry, biblical studies, and English. In fact, regardless of the field of study, much of the educational process involves students listening to faculty lectures. It naturally follows that those who learn to listen effectively earn better grades.

In addition, an increasing number of college-level classes require individual or group presentations. Using effective public speaking skills makes such presentations much more effective. On presentation assignments, those who have compelling speeches that are well researched and effectively delivered will invariably gain better grades.

Further, many college-level classes require a research paper. The same skills that enable a student to do research for an effective speech presentation can also be applied to research papers in Bible survey, biology, or art appreciation. Those who master these research techniques are therefore more likely to get high marks on research projects in all of their courses.

Reason #3 Sharpened Leadership Skills

Americans tend to equate leadership with the ability to talk well in public.[2] For example, former Secretary of State Colin Powell was widely regarded by members of both political parties in the United States, and by leaders around the world, as an effective international leader. People drew that conclusion about Powell partially because of his skill as an orator.

Similarly, in the world of business, CEOs are often called upon to address stockholders, managers, or customers. It is simply assumed that one in such a high position of leadership will excel in public address as well. Public speaking is so vital to a business leader's success that a growing number of companies employ ghostwriters to help executives in this critical area. Corporate leaders may choose to polish their speaking skill at such training grounds as Decker Communication in San Francisco or Executive Techniques in Chicago. These giants in the public speaking training industry reportedly command very high daily fees for personalized training sessions for executives.[3]

The same correlation between leadership and public address is evidenced in the church. Many consider Billy Graham a leader of the evangelical Christian community. Much of that profile is attributable to the fact that through public address Graham has effectively persuaded thousands to follow Christ. Since he is successful in public speaking, he is therefore looked to as a leader.

Mayors may be called upon to address the citizenry on behalf of a park proposal. Candidates, expecting to be elected to student council, speak to the student body with a clear and convincing appeal for votes. Sunday school teachers engage their class with the truth of the Biblical

---

2. Roach and Wyatt, *Successful Listening*, 21.
3. Litfin, *Public Speaking*, 34.

message and a plan for its application. In each case, leadership success is closely tied to public speaking skill.

Clearly, there exists a strong correlation between public speaking ability and leadership. As a result, those who successfully master the skills taught in a public speaking class can expect to also enjoy a multitude of leadership opportunities.

Reason #4 Service to Others

The reasons for studying public speaking examined thus far are all arguably self oriented. Reason four by contrast looks beyond the self to the needs of others. Christians are called to love others and care for the oppressed.[4] Sometimes this calling requires speaking publicly on behalf of those who are treated unjustly. Quentin Schultze uses the term "servant speakers" to point out this important purpose of public speaking.[5]

The Old Testament book of Exodus records one of the earliest speech assignments in history, when in chapter three God instructs Moses to prepare a speech to be delivered to Pharaoh. The purpose of the speech is to facilitate the freedom of the people of Israel. God clearly reveals to Moses that the oppression of the people of Israel has prompted the calling of a servant speaker.[6]

William Wilberforce, one of the best known of the English abolitionists, was also a servant speaker. At only twenty-one Wilberforce was elected to Parliament. Even then he was recognized for his eloquence. But only after an evangelical conversion did he choose to use his speaking skills for the benefit of slaves and others who could not speak for themselves.[7] Wilberforce continued as a servant speaker for twenty years, finally winning the fight to end the slave trade on February 23, 1807.[8]

A more recent servant speaker was the Roman Catholic nun and founder of the Missionaries of Charity, Mother Teresa. She was awarded the Nobel Peace prize in 1979 for her work among the lepers of Calcutta. In her Nobel speech she declared, "I feel that the passion of Christ is being

---

4. See for example Micah 6:8 and I John 4:7.
5. Schultze, *An Essential Guide*, 11.
6. See Exodus 3:7–9.
7. Carey, "William Wilberforce (1759–1833)," http://www.brycchancarey.com/abolition/wilberforce.htm.
8. Abraham, "Let My People Go," 17–19.

relived all over again—and we are to share that passion, to share the sufferings of people."⁹ Clearly Mother Teresa saw herself as a servant speaker.

Reason #5 Historic Mainstream

Public speaking is one of the oldest of the academic disciplines. In ancient days the study was called *rhetoric*, and practitioners of public address were known as *rhetoricians*. The ancient philosopher Aristotle is often referred to as the "father of rhetoric." In his book entitled *Rhetoric*, written more than 2000 years ago, he offered three forms of proof including logos, pathos, and ethos. These three continue to be the foundation for much of what comprises a standard public speaking course today. In fact, scholars still consider Aristotle's work one of the most important public speaking textbooks ever written.

> *Aristotle:* Father of rhetoric, who wrote a book entitled Rhetoric in the fourth century B. C.

Later, the Apostles used public address to accomplish their evangelistic purpose. For example according to Acts 17, in his speech in the Areopagus of Athens, Paul helped transform a city for the cause of Jesus Christ. And Stephen had undoubtedly influenced Saul earlier with his death-defying proclamation of the truth of the resurrection reported in Acts 7.

In more recent times, the impact of public address has grown as a result of the eloquence of leaders like Winston Churchill, John Kennedy, Martin Luther King Jr., Margaret Thatcher, and Ronald Reagan. These leaders and others like them have renewed the world's interest in effective oratory. A student's completion of a public speaking course enables full participation in this worldwide rhetorical revival. To study public speaking is to participate in the historic mainstream.

Reason #6 Life Preparation

On a college campus somewhere in America today there is enrolled a student who will some day deliver his or her inaugural address as president of the United States. Another will give a speech accepting a Grammy or an Oscar. Still another will speak to a press conference about an international corporate acquisition. And yet another will address thousands around the world from a televised evangelistic crusade. Hence those taking a public

---

9. Cited in Ackerman, *Great Souls*, 239.

speaking class this semester are preparing for these potential real-life scenarios and others like them.

Of course, not just famous world leaders do public speaking. Sometimes the spotlight of the public arena shines upon common and everyday men and women. That was the case for Jessica Lynch, an army reservist who gained celebrity as a prisoner of war during the liberation of Iraq. Once rescued, Jessica addressed a crowd of thousands of well wishers at a gathering in her hometown of Palestine, West Virginia. She had precious little preparation for the demands of that day. "Her mother and father say a lot of people forget that Jessi left Palestine as a just graduated high school senior who had never seen much of the world . . . Jessi had never made a speech outside English class. Now she was making one covered by Swedish television, British newspapers, and NPR."[10]

Clearly, Jessica was thrust into the spotlight by the circumstances of real life. While audience members reported that her speech proved effective, it undoubtedly would have been easier for her to accomplish that high quality result if she had already successfully completed a college-level public speaking course.

Reason #7 Career Preparation

One study asked former students which of the skills that they had developed in college they now believed were the most essential in improving career effectiveness.[11] Those former students placed skills in oral communication at the top of their list. Public speaking specifically rated very high. Those former students know that public speaking is an important part of many professions and careers.

That also explains why employers consistently search for employees who have mastered communication skills. In a study, conducted by the National Association of Colleges and Employers and reported in the Wall Street Journal, the ability to communicate ranked first among the personal qualities sought by an employer.[12] This study involved four hundred and eighty companies and public organizations.

In a similar study, a random sampling of one thousand human resource managers were asked their opinion about the factors most impor-

---

10. Bragg, *I Am A Soldier, Too*, 191.
11. Zekeri, "College Curriculum Competencies," 412–23.
12. Karr, "A Special News Report."

tant to college graduates searching for employment. Once again, at the top of the list was "oral communication skills."[13]

Employers are searching for effective communicators because they recognize communication as a vital part of almost every career position. For example, one study discovered that the ability to communicate proves vital for those involved in business careers.[14] In a similar finding, 76 percent of executives reported having to give oral reports as a routine part of their work assignment.[15]

Increasingly, nurses are called upon to give public presentations as part of their work.[16] As a result, leaders in that field encourage nurse trainees to take the necessary steps to minimize the fear of public speaking.

It is generally thought that accountants work with data rather than with people. However, researchers also report that men and women in that field benefit greatly from the development of communication skills.[17]

Teachers must also know how to communicate in order to accomplish their work effectively. It is reported that secondary teachers and undergraduate education faculty list communication courses as more important than others in the preparation of effective teachers for the classroom.[18]

Whether teacher, preacher, industrialist, business leader, politician, engineer, accountant, or architect, the ability to effectively address an audience will strengthen and support a professional career. Often those who have mastered the art of public speaking later achieve the greatest success in their chosen profession.

Reason #8 Increased General Knowledge

In most public speaking classes, participants have the opportunity to serve as audience members for their colleague student-speakers. Listening carefully to classroom speeches provides exposure to a great deal of information on a variety of subjects. As a result participation in such a class offers the serendipitous benefit of enhancing general knowledge. Recently, during just one

---

13. Curtis, et al., "National Preferences," 6–14.
14. Maes, et al., "A Managerial Perspective," 67–80.
15. Wyllie, "Oral Communication," 15.
16. Bates, "Unaccustomed," 25–27.
17. Stinson and Asquith, "Excellent Communication Skills," 385–90; Stowers and White, "Connecting Accounting and Communication," 23–31.
18. Johnson and Roelke, "Secondary Teachers' and Undergraduate Education Faculty," 127–38.

semester of public speaking at a small Christian liberal arts college, students heard speeches on:

- Ethical issues surrounding stem cell research
- The pros and cons of capital punishment
- The advantages of taking a two-week mission trip
- Growing up in the Bahamas
- The ministry of Mother Teresa
- The life of Mahatma Gandhi
- Selecting the equipment necessary for a first sky dive
- How to develop an investment portfolio
- The importance of daily devotions
- Setting up your own Web page
- Administering CPR
- The causes and cures of anorexia
- The basics of good nutrition
- How to wrestle an alligator

Obviously, the information exchanged in this public speaking class went well beyond the skills of public speaking. Because of exposure to so many speeches on contemporary issues and current events, students of public speaking often become among the most knowledgeable and best-informed people on their campus.

Reason #9 Response to Biblical Command

For the Christian, one of the most important reasons to study public speaking involves responding to the clear command of Scripture. I Peter 3:15 instructs "Always be prepared to give an answer to everyone who asks you to give the reason for the hope that you have" (NIV). While many believers welcome an opportunity to share their faith in a one-on-one or small group setting, those same Christians may feel less comfortable proclaiming the truth of Christ in a larger gathering. Yet the terms "always" and "everyone" in this important verse indicate that the setting should never be allowed to impede the proclamation of the truth.

The senior adult group of a local church invited Matt to give his testimony. He refused the invitation. "I didn't know how to give a testimony speech," he explained. "I was certain that I would embarrass myself in front of all of those older people."

The local Lion's Club in her community selected Jennie as a scholarship recipient. Along with the award came the responsibility of addressing the organization in order to express appreciation. "I wanted to explain what Christ had done for me and why I choose to use the award to attend a Christian university," she recalled. "But at that point I simply didn't know how to work that into my speech."

The Campus Director of Spiritual Life asked Brooke to report on her summer mission's experience in Ukraine during a regular chapel service. She sensed that God wanted her to accept the invitation, but instead she reluctantly declined. She just could not envision herself overcoming her natural anxiety in order to address the entire student body.

Matt, Jennie, and Brooke later took a public speaking course together. Their instructor declared I Peter 3:15 to be the rationale for the entire semester. As a result of that class, the trio agreed that they were much better prepared to respond effectively to public speaking invitations. That was especially true when those invitations included the opportunity to proclaim their faith in Jesus Christ. They have learned the power of proclamation. Mastery of that power begins with an understanding of how the communication process works.

Communication Settings

The word *communication* comes from the Latin word communicare, meaning "to share" or "to participate." It is the act of imparting, conferring, or delivering knowledge, opinions, or facts from one individual to another. The study of communication is generally divided into five distinct settings. While there are many similarities in each of these settings, they differ in the number of people involved and the nature and immediacy of feedback.

> *Communication*: The act of imparting, conferring, or delivering knowledge, opinions, or facts from one individual to another.

Intrapersonal Communication

Intrapersonal communication is communication within oneself. It represents the most basic form of communication since it involves only one individual. It is, in reality, dialoging internally. Many experts define intrapersonal communication simply as thinking.

During a classmate's speech, Becca found herself daydreaming about her plans for a weekend date. She had momentarily abandoned her responsibilities as a listener at the public speaking level of communication in order to engage in intrapersonal communication.

Stan's mental analysis of whether to do his speech to inform on the authorship of the book of Hebrews or on the biblical concept of tithing represents a form of intrapersonal communication. However, if Stan asks Marcia for her opinion he has moved to another setting of communication called interpersonal communication.

Interpersonal Communication

Interpersonal communication is communication that occurs between two people. The study of this setting of communication is sometimes referred to as *dyadic communication* since the word *dyad* is derived from the Latin for "pair." Interpersonal communication explores the components of conversation. But interpersonal communication goes beyond mere conversation. Many experts view interpersonal communication as the study of relationships. Interpersonal communication considers how relationships grow and how they disintegrate. It may also explore such topics as trust, power, conflict resolution, and listening. In addition, a class in interpersonal communication often includes an introduction into the ways people communicate nonverbally.

Group Communication

Adding to the number of people involved in a communication setting leads to the study of *group communication*. Researchers generally agree that the dynamics of group communication come into play when three or more people interact in the pursuit of a common goal. Participants in such a group accept particular *roles* within the group. Those roles may include informal responsibilities for group development or task accomplishment.

Group norms, or rules for behavior, also develop within on-going groups. For example, the student union roundtable group that was introduced at the beginning of this chapter might begin to eat lunch while they study public speaking together. Without even having a discussion, a norm may emerge that involves getting lunch before coming to the table, rather than waiting on the entire group. *Norms* are the unspoken rules for appropriate or inappropriate behavior in group-life.

The study of group member roles and group norms is an important part of the study of small group communication. A class in group communication also usually includes the development of group cohesion through various phases of group life.

Public Speaking

Public speaking, the subject of this book, involves communication from one speaker to many listeners in the context of a face-to-face setting. Public address, or rhetoric, was the first of the five settings of communication to be formally studied. As previously noted, an early major writing on the subject was by Aristotle of Athens in the fourth century BC. Speakers use public address today for everything from persuading voters to informing classes. It occurs as the preferred communication level for building up the body of Christ and for toasting newlyweds. A grandchild uses public speaking to eulogize a grandfather and a CEO uses it to convince stockholders. Clearly, public speaking remains an important component of modern American life.

> *Public speaking*: Communication from one speaker to many listeners in a face to face setting

Mass Communication

An audience so large or geographically disconnected that it cannot be engaged in face-to-face communication becomes part of a fifth setting of communication: *mass communication*. Mass communication focuses on the means of message transmission. Television, radio, the World Wide Web, or print media all may be employed in order to communicate to a wider audience. The element of feedback is usually delayed, and may even be eliminated in mass communication. Still, modern culture is moving decidedly toward this broader but less personal form of communication.

Sometimes public speaking and mass communication are blended in a unique rhetorical event. On one occasion, for example, Billy Graham reports having spoken to forty-nine thousand people face to face, while another thirty thousand watched on large-screen closed-circuit television from a remote site, and more than one hundred million viewers watched on television from their homes.[19]

Elements of Communication

Each of these settings of communication has unique characteristics, yet the basic elements comprising the communication process are recogniz-

---

19. Graham, *Storm Warnings*, 311.

able in each of the five. These elements include sender, message, channel, receiver, feedback, and noise.

Sender

The *sender*, or source of communication, places thoughts, ideas, or emotions into a form which can be understood by another through the process of encoding. The sender may encode into either a verbal or nonverbal form.

At the public speaking level, the speaker is the sender. The speaker may work for several weeks, or even months, on researching ideas and putting them into just the right words. The most effective public speakers recognize that hand gestures, facial expressions, and body movements also play an important role in the encoding process. In addition, the speaker may find it appropriate to use a specialized form of encoding called a visual aid in the speech.

Message

Messages are written, spoken, or unspoken symbols to which two or more people assign meaning. Words represent the most common form of message, but nonverbal signs and signals are also messages. Senders may encode messages either intentionally or unintentionally. In public speaking the message includes the text of the speech and all of the associated nonverbal elements of the delivery.

Channel

A message travels from a sender to a receiver via some pathway called a *channel*. Senders both knowingly and unknowingly transmit messages through a variety of channels. Senders sometimes engage more than one channel simultaneously. For example, a sender who makes a strong point verbally may also reinforce the message by means of voice inflection or an appropriate gesture. In doing so that sender has used both a verbal and a nonverbal channel.

In public speaking speech delivery becomes the channel. Speakers may employ one of a variety of delivery styles. The best public speakers select the right delivery style for their intended purpose and then practice repeatedly in order to use that style with maximum effectiveness.

Receiver

The receiver decodes the message from the sender and attempts to understand the sender's intent. To the extent that the receiver and sender agree on the meaning of the messages or symbols used, there is an understanding sometimes referred to as a *meeting of the minds*. Usually, however, the message as decoded differs to some degree from the message encoded by the sender. In other words, at least a portion of the intent of the sender has been lost. A complete meeting of the minds is rarely, if ever, accomplished.

> *Meeting of the Minds*: Agreement that exists between a sender and a receiver on the meaning of the symbols comprising a message.

In public speaking the audience plays the part of the receiver. Actually, the audience represents a group of receivers that the sender or speaker addresses simultaneously. In order to assist the audience in effective decoding, the speaker engages in *audience analysis* during preparation. Audience analysis is the process by which the sender anticipates the receiver in public speaking. Effective speakers strive to help the audience maximize the meeting of the minds.

Feedback

Sometimes a sender and receiver switch roles in order to facilitate the encoding of a response message. Such a response message is called *feedback*. As with any message, the feedback message may be verbal or nonverbal, intentional or unintentional.

In a public speaking setting, the feedback usually comes to a speaker from the audience by means of nonverbal messages. A puzzled look, for example, may tell a speaker that the point has not been communicated effectively. A knowing nod of the head sends the opposite message. A shaking of the head may signal disagreement, while a smile may communicate understanding. In other situations, feedback comes in the form of an interruption to the speaker. For example, a raised hand signals that an audience member wants to gain acknowledgment and ask a question. In still other cases, the feedback comes after the speech. Such forms of *post-address feedback* include comments like "that was a great speech" or "you really got me thinking about that topic."

> *Post-Address Feedback*: Comments about a speech that are directed to the speaker after the speech is over.

Noise

Noise is anything that keeps a message from being understood as a sender intended. Noise usually takes one of three forms:

1. *Environmental noise* is the noise that comes from surroundings and interrupts effective communication flow.

2. *Physiological noise* exists within the physical being of the sender or the receiver. This may include hearing impairment in the receiver. It might also take the form of a speech impediment or accent in the sender.

3. *Psychological noise* is the noise that occurs in the minds of either the sender or the receiver. Worry about some circumstance extraneous to the current communication is a common example.

In public speaking all three of the forms of noise can have impact. A room that is too hot or too cold to allow concentration may provide environmental noise. So, too, does an open window allowing traffic noise into the room or a noisy air-conditioning unit in an enclosed environment. Physiological noise can interrupt a public speaking situation when an after-dinner speaker tries to keep an audience awake after a heavy meal or when the speaker and audience do not share the same first language. Finally, psychological noise may occur when an audience member succumbs to daydreaming instead of paying careful attention to the speech, or when a speaker focuses on his or her anxiety rather than on the delivery of the speech.

A discussion of the elements of communication serve to provide some understanding of the process, but, in reality, they offer an oversimplified view. Communication is a complex, ever-changing process that is difficult to reduce to a few pages. In fact, the public speaking process is better experienced than read about. That is why the pages that follow are designed to quickly move the student of public speaking on to the exciting moment of proclamation.

The Chapter in Brief

There are at least nine good reasons, beyond the typical "It's required," to study public speaking. These include:

- Enhanced relationships
- Improved academic standing
- Sharpened leadership skills
- Service to others
- Historic mainstream
- Life preparation
- Career preparation
- Increased general knowledge
- Response to biblical command

Public speaking, the subject of this text, is just one of the settings of communication that human beings participate in. The other settings include intrapersonal, interpersonal, group, and mass communication.

Each of the settings of communication involves a sender encoding ideas into a message. That message is transmitted along a channel to a receiver, who then decodes and interprets the message. The response of the receiver to the sender's original message is sent in the same manner and is known as feedback. Noise is anything interfering with the process, thus making communication less effective.

Key Terms

Use the list below to test your knowledge of the vocabulary introduced in this chapter.

- communication
- Aristotle
- intrapersonal communication
- post-address feedback
- interpersonal communication
- group communication
- norms
- roles
- public speaking
- mass communication
- sender
- message
- receiver

- channel
- feedback
- environmental noise
- rhetoric
- meeting of the minds
- audience analysis
- psychological noise
- physiological noise

For Review and Discussion

1. Cynthia asked the roundtable discussion group, "Why do we have to take public speaking?" How would you now answer her question? Which of the nine reasons do you personally find the most motivating? Why?

2. Make a list of careers and professions that appear to never require public speaking. Interview people who work at those careers or are members of those professions to test your assumptions. How prevalent is public speaking in the work-a-day world?

3. Interview a member of your intended career or profession in order to determine the role of public speaking in the work you will be doing.

Proclamation Practice

Prepare, for delivery in class, a two to three minute speech explaining how communication works.

2

From the Other Side of the Lectern

Chapter Challenges

A careful reading of Chapter 2 will provide insight into these chapter challenges:

1. How important is listening in America today?
2. How effectively do most Americans listen?
3. List the four purposes of listening.
4. Describe six keys to improved listening.

At the Student Union Roundtable

"That was an awesome presentation," declared Ryan as he slid into his chair at the student union roundtable. The public speaking study group was gathering in the student union after chapel.

"It certainly was very informative," said Janelle. "I had no idea there were so many from our campus involved in summer ministries. Think of it, 75% of our student body was involved in missions during the past summer."

"It was a great chapel. I liked how all those students who were involved in summer ministry shared their experiences," agreed Cynthia. "I distinctly remember hearing the figure 37%, though. That's still a very good number."

"You're both wrong," Belsa chimed in. "Dr. Ray, the campus pastor spoke of every person on our campus being involved in ministry. Every— that means 100%, not 75%, not 37%."

There arose a loud and animated discussion over how many people from the campus participated in summer ministry. Four members of the round table group each seemed to have heard a different figure. Finally, Cynthia turned to Jess, the only quiet member of the group thus far. "What did you hear?" she asked.

With a smile Jess answered, "37% were involved in overseas ministry. 75% were involved in some ministry either domestic or overseas. And Dr. Ray has set a goal that 100% be involved in summer ministry next year. In addition, it sounds as if 100% of this group better plan to attend public speaking class next hour. The lecture is on becoming a better listener."

The Importance of Listening

Jess is right. The roundtable study group will undoubtedly benefit from instruction in listening. The group's listening problems, however, are not unique. One listening expert writes, "Listening is so basic we take it for granted. Unfortunately, most of us think of ourselves as better listeners than we really are."[1] That opinion is supported in a study noting that average listeners think that they recall 75–80% of what they hear, while in fact their actual recollection is only 25%.[2]

This ineffective listening means serious problems for businesses since at least 75% of the average employee's workday is spent in communication,

---

1. Nichols, *Lost Art*, 11.
2. Roach and Wyatt, "Listening and Rhetorical Process," 171–76.

with up to half of that time spent engaged in listening.[3] Some experts on listening put the figure at closer to 60% of employee time given to the task of listening.[4] But, the precise figure is less important than the realization that listening is an important part of the workday for many employees.

Success guru Jack Canfield declares that effective listening is an important key to success beyond the world of business.[5] He believes that listening insures accuracy and fairness in relationships. Others declare that poor listening leads to a deterioration of relationships in general and an increase in marital failure in particular.[6]

Perhaps one of the most important results of listening ineffectiveness stems from the correlation between listening and academic success. Since a large portion of classroom time is spent listening, better students are usually better listeners. One study discovered that college students spent 53 percent of their total communication time listening.[7] A similar study, which focused on class time only, discovered that nearly 90 percent of a college student's time while in class is spent listening.[8] A student who listens poorly, therefore, is less than effective during the major block of time spent in academic pursuits.

The roundtable group would discover that postponing their discussion about chapel for a few hours would yield even greater comprehension problems. Most people initially remember only a small percentage of what they hear, and to compound the problem, as much as 90 percent of that information will not be retained in the long run[9]. Experts agree that immediately after listening to a speech, an audience member recalls only 50 percent of what was said. But, forty-eight hours later the retained information has been sliced in half again. In two days an audience member recalls only 25 percent of the original information.[10] Clearly there is a great need for improved listening.

Public speaking class provides a marvelous opportunity to practice listening skills and thus improve listening performance. Suppose the instructor of a public speaking class requires each student to deliver four

3. Alessandra, *Charisma*, 113.
4. Wolvin and Coakley, "*Survey of Status*," 152–64.
5. Canfield, *Success Principles*, 325–29.
6. Wolvin and Coakley, *Listening*, 19.
7. Barker et al., "*Investigation of Proportional Time*," 101–9.
8. Coakley and Wolvin, "*Listening in Education Environment*," 179–212.
9. Bostrom and Bryant, "*Factors in Retention*," 137–45.
10. Steil et al., *Effective Listening*, 38

speeches. And suppose further that the class has twenty-five students. That means, during the course of the semester, a particular student listens to ninety-six speeches while delivering just four. Perhaps the class should be renamed "Listening Lab." At any rate, the typical public speaking class provides an excellent opportunity to hone listening skills.

Listening Purposes

Just as a speaker must establish the purpose of the speech early in the speech development process, so too must a listener establish the purpose for listening. Listening generally fits into one of four purposes.

Appreciative Listening

The first purpose of listening is *appreciative listening*, or listening simply for enjoyment. Often appreciative listening is associated with music appreciation. But appreciative listening can also extend to a great movie or a well-delivered speech. Some listeners also appreciate the sounds of nature, the sounds of a small child at play, or the sound of a well-tuned machine.

Empathetic Listening

The second type of listening, *empathetic listening,* is sometimes called "therapeutic listening." Empathetic listening involves listening to the concerns of another in order to provide emotional support. From time to time most people serve as an empathetic listener for a friend or associate. The best empathetic listeners resist the temptation to offer quick advice. Instead they listen with compassion and understanding, helping the speaker formulate his or her own solutions.

The book of Job offers a case study on the need for empathetic listening. When life dealt Job some serious blows, his friends gathered around. Over and over, those friends offered advice and devised solutions designed to fit Job's situation and meet his needs. Finally, Job had enough. He appealed in Job 21:1, "Listen carefully to my words. Let this be the consolation you give me" (NIV). Job's words might accurately be paraphrased, "Be quiet and listen! Let that be your ministry."

Job is not alone in his appeal. Thousands in America today echo his words. The need for empathetic listeners has never been greater.

Comprehensive Listening

A third purpose of listening, *comprehensive listening* involves listening for understanding while withholding judgment. The comprehensive listener seeks to gain a complete understanding of the speaker's intended message. Since much of the educational process includes hearing lectures and responding with the appropriate information on an exam, comprehensive listening is especially important to college students. The public speaking class provides a forum for developing comprehensive listening skills through careful technique and persistent practice.

Those seeking to develop comprehensive listening skills do so by listening for the main ideas. Listeners who can correctly list the thesis statement of a speech have usually begun doing an adequate job of comprehensive listening. In addition to thesis identification, effective comprehensive listeners listen for the structure of the speech or lecture. Good listeners find it possible to list at least the main points addressed by the speaker. Comprehensive listeners also train themselves to listen for the supporting evidence of the speech. They absorb the illustrations, statistics, and testimony statements that develop the main points and make it memorable.

Critical Listening

A fourth type of listening, *critical listening*, involves going beyond simply hearing and comprehending a speaker's message. The critical listener also evaluates the speaker's words. In the case of good listeners critical does not mean negative in approach. Instead critical listeners are objective, carefully examining a speaker's message and point of view, evaluating the strengths and weaknesses of the message.

Media consumption is one important use of critical listening. Advertisers constantly bombard audiences with messages. As a result, citizens in a free society also act as consumers of public address. Effective critical listeners seek to evaluate the comparative claims of these professional persuaders.

The rise of Nazi Germany during the years leading up to World War II provides a case study in the dangers of ineffective critical listening. Modern Americans find it difficult to understand how Germans in the 1930s could have listened to the words of the eloquent Adolf Hitler without raising some serious questions about his disturbing views. Yet critical listening is also important in twenty-first-century America.

Keys to Improved Listening

With so many advantages to quality listening, many people have a real desire to become better listeners. Six keys to improved listening will assist in that endeavor.

Key #1 Listen Ethically

Just like speakers, audience members have ethical responsibilities associated with listening. Ethical listeners demonstrate respect for the speaker by paying careful attention. Even if a topic seems uninteresting or a speaker's point of view differs from the listener's own, the ethical listener continues to pay attention. The word *attention* literally means "a collection of tensions." That meaning implies that sometimes the listening task is difficult.

Ethical listeners also avoid reacting to superficial qualities in a speaker or a speech. A listener who gets hung up on a speaker's attire, or the topic or title of the address, may miss the important substance of the speech. Of course, speakers should look professional and avoid words that distract in the title or topic of the speech. However, a speaker who fails to perform effectively does not issue audience members a license for ineffective and unethical listening.

Still further, ethical listeners give the speaker the benefit of the doubt. Some positions that seem wrong are actually just outside the immediate frame of reference of the listener. Therefore the ethical listener withholds judgment and gives the speaker the benefit of the doubt on questions arising out of a speech.

Finally, ethical listeners hold questions until the appropriate time. Audience members may sometimes help a speaker by raising a question for clarification. However, most speakers prefer that listeners hold questions until the end of the point, perhaps even until the end of the speech. Ethical listeners then ask their questions succinctly, avoiding the temptation to filibuster or launch into a speech on an opposing viewpoint.

Key #2 Use the Entire Listening Process

Many audience members find their listening enhanced when they recognize the differences between listening and hearing. Hearing is the physiological process of obtaining sound waves through the ears. Listening on the other hand, involves a multi-faceted process, including the search for meaning and application. While experts disagree on the totality of the process,[11] it remains clear that at the very least listening encompasses four important steps.

> *Listening*: The process of hearing, attending, comprehending, and remembering.

- Hearing
- Attending
- Comprehending
- Remembering

Hearing, the first step in the listening process, results from the complex physiological process whereby the human ear translates air pressure variations into electrical impulses, which are in turn transmitted to the brain via the auditory nerve.

> *Hearing*: Physiological process of obtaining sound waves through the ears.

Modern technology makes it possible for the hearing impaired to compensate for physical auditory limitations. But technology does not compensate for poor listening. Good listeners recognize that hearing is only the first step in the listening process.

Sounds may be heard and recorded by the brain of a person who pays no attention to those sounds. Since the average person is exposed to hundreds of sounds every day, he or she must choose which sounds to pay attention to. That selection is called attending and is the second step of the listening process.

Many college freshmen report difficulty studying or sleeping during their first few days in a dormitory. They note that the noise level is much higher than what they are used to. Later in the semester, the noise persists, yet the same students develop the ability to tune it out and function normally. Over time they have learned how to more effectively focus their attention and select only the sounds they find interesting or beneficial. Such selective listening can lead to problems, however, when those same students sit in class and inadvertently tune out a lecture or the announcement of an important assignment.

---

11. Halone et al., "Toward Establishment," 12–28.

Since attending is a matter of decision, the effective listener consciously evaluates the benefits of paying attention. Such an evaluation can be accomplished by asking oneself prior to a speech, "What must I do to get physically and mentally ready to listen?" Another attention focusing question is "What are the benefits to me of paying attention to this speaker?"

> *Attending*: Second step in the listening process that involves deciding what to pay attention to.

The third step in the listening process, *comprehending*, is the point at which good listeners are separated from the mainstream. These good listeners know that without comprehension all the hearing and paying attention to a speech has been wasted. These effective listeners therefore raise questions when appropriate, wrestle mentally with the presentation, compare and contrast points, and do whatever else is necessary to comprehend the meaning of a speech.

> *Comprehending*: The third step in the listening process that involves understanding the meaning of the message.

The best listeners recognize that the details are usually not as important as the main ideas. They first listen for the thesis statement and for the main points of a speaker's speech. Only after grasping that main idea do they search for the material presented in the supporting structure. As a result, they usually find supporting material easier to comprehend and remember.

The fourth and final step of the listening process is remembering. Information heard, selected for attention, and understood must later be recalled in order for the listening to have been deemed effective. A host of researchers have analyzed the physiological process of memory and offer suggestions for improved information retention.[12]

---

12. See for example: Tileston, *What Every Teacher Should Know*; Baddeley, *Your Memory*; Schacter, *Seven Sins of Memory*.

> *Remembering*: Fourth and final step in the listening process that involves the ability to recall what has been heard.

Key #3 Delay Evaluation

Today's North Americans live in an instantaneous society. Everything from electronic communication to ATM banking to microwave cooking provides overwhelming evidence that moderns hate to wait. Participants in this culture of the immediate expect and demand instant gratification for every conceivable need or desire.

Problems arise, however, when the instantaneous mentality is carried into the world of communication. Whether at the level of interpersonal, group, or public communication, some receivers become so skilled at instant communication that they find it totally unnecessary to hear an entire message before beginning the process of evaluation and response formulation. In fact, sometimes a communicator can determine a response on the basis of a single word. Words that trigger such a response are referred to as emotion-laden words.

> *Emotion laden words*: Words that trigger an emotional response in a listener often short-circuiting the listening process.

In a speech on the marketing of soft drinks, a midwestern student-speaker continually referred to the product by the regional term "pop." An audience member from southern Georgia later admitted she had heard very little of the content of the speech. "That Yankee just kept calling it 'pop' instead of 'Coke,'" she fumed. "It's like fingers on a blackboard to me."

In a self-introduction speech in a state university public speaking class, a Christian was able to weave his testimony into the assigned speech. The speech might have been well received except that he repeatedly referred to non-believers as "pagans." Most of his audience failed to listen beyond, what was for them, his emotion-laden terminology.

The best listeners realize that they will from time to time hear words or phrases that trigger an internal emotional response. These good listeners, however, use the emotion-laden word as a reminder to intensify their listening efforts. They recognize words as vehicles, designed to convey messages. Good listeners know that the message is much more important than the vehicle that bears the message.

Sometimes it is not an emotion-laden word but an entire concept or thesis statement that threatens to cause an ineffective listener to jump to conclusions. In a speech to persuade delivered on a Christian college campus, a student attempted to convince her audience that "a woman's right to choose is an important constitutional guarantee that must be protected." Her mostly evangelical and decidedly pro-life audience did not agree with her thesis.

Some in the audience, however, were good listeners, who delayed their evaluations. These good listeners mentally responded, "That sounds contrary to moral thinking to me. I wonder what would cause a person to make such a statement. Let me see if I can understand her position."

Others in the same audience rushed quickly to judgment. Mentally they declared, "That is absurd. She must not even be a Christian. The Bible says God knew each of us in our mother's womb. What else is there to say on the subject?"

Key #4 Use Thought Speed Effectively

On average, an audience member has the capacity to think at a speed of 400–800 words per minute, while the average speaker delivers a speech at the rate of only 120–150 words per minute.[13] This difference, sometimes called "leftover thinking space,"[14] means that an audience member can process more than twice the verbal stimuli being offered by a speaker. This thought speed to speech speed difference provides the single greatest liability to public speaking listening.

One needs only consider the thought speed to reading speed difference that plagues many college students in order to recognize the nature of the problem. Students without the benefit of training in speed-reading usually read at a much slower rate than the rate at which they think. This allows ample time for mental excursions during reading.

---

13. Wolvin and Coakley, *Listening*, 207.
14. Lundsteen, "*Metacognitive Listening*," 106–123.

> *Thought speed*: Rate at which an audience member thinks, typically four hundred to eight hundred words per minute.
>
> *Speech speed*: Rate at which a speaker talks, typically one hundred twenty to one hundred fifty words per minute.

For example, Stacy discovered when she had completed reading the first chapter of her public speaking book that she really didn't understand what she had read. That was because she had thought about several other topics while she read. She had in effect used her excess brain time to become totally occupied with a mental side trip. Physiologically her eyes followed the words on the printed page, but mentally she engaged in other matters.

A similar thing happens to an audience member who uses excess brain time to think about matters other than the subject of the speech. Eventually that listener discovers that he or she has effectively tuned out the entire speech.

A good listener, by contrast, uses the thought speed to speech speed difference for several important tasks designed to enhance comprehension and retention.

1. Review previous points. The effective listener stays on topic by reviewing repeatedly the speaker's main points.

2. Anticipate future points. The good listener anticipates the speaker's next points. When that listener anticipates correctly, repetition aids retention. When a different point emerges than anticipated, then the listener learns by comparing and contrasting.

3. Evaluate the speaker's position. The good listener uses his or her excess brain time to perform preliminary evaluation of the speaker's points, delivery, and positions.

Key #5 Minimize Distractions

External distractions often keep an audience member from being an effective listener. The best listeners have learned to minimize the impact of these external distractions.

- Mandi found the room where public speaking class was held to be uncomfortably cold. On speech days she discovered that warmer attire made her a better listener.

- Curtis struggled to stay awake during speeches. The problem was magnified because he ate lunch the hour prior to the class. Postponing lunch made him a better listener.
- Since her public speaking classroom lacked sound amplification, Courtney found herself struggling to hear some of the speeches. She moved to the front of the room and became a better listener.
- Jose struggled to be a good listener in part because Dan, who sat beside him, commented on the speeches under his breath. When Jose moved away from Dan, his listening effectiveness improved.
- Carol discovered that sitting near the window on a sunny day diverted her attention to the activities outside on the campus lawn. Moving to the opposite side of the room improved her listening.

In each of these cases, listening improved because students correctly evaluated their own susceptibility to external distraction and took appropriate corrective actions. They recognized that good listening demanded the minimization of distractions.

Key #6 Take Effective Notes

Many students argue that taking notes distracts from effective listening. They maintain that they can only focus on one activity at a time. In fact, the opposite is usually true.[15] The process of taking notes focuses the attention on the subject matter and thus enhances listening as well as retention. Some practical tips for note taking include:

1. Be prepared. Coming to a class lecture or speech with pencil and paper ready for note taking prepares the mind for attention. Good listeners assume that notes will be necessary.
2. Use a two-column system. While there are several effective notetaking systems, one of the best is the two-column approach. Effective listeners use only one column of their notetaking paper during the speech or lecture. The second column remains for later edits. These adjustments may come from rereading the text or from reviewing a colleague's notes on the same lecture or speech.
3. Write main points first. Listen and record the main points of a speech first. Details can be added later if necessary.

---

15. Titsworth, "Effects of Teacher Immediacy," 283–97.

4. Paraphrase. Don't try to write a speaker's phraseology word for word. Instead, put the ideas into familiar terms.
5. Be brief. The fewer words the better in good notes. The notes should just incorporate the important ideas of the speech.
6. Postpone grammar and spell-check. Record the notes as quickly and efficiently as possible. Rewriting later not only cleans up the finished notes, but allows for review as well.
7. Write down questions. As the speech or lecture develops the note taker may encounter questions for follow-up either with the speaker or in future study. These questions are a part of the notetaking process for the effective listener.
8. Organize the notes. Having notes is one thing—having them in a usable form for quick reference is quite another. Using a loose-leaf notebook, for example, will allow for the substitution of pertinent information at a later point.
9. Review the notes. Since retention is the objective, and it is also the greatest barrier to listening success, the most effective listeners review notes periodically following the lecture or speech.

The Chapter in Brief

A tremendous need exists for more effective listening among communicators. Most people rate themselves as a much better listener than the evidence supports. Part of the problem is a failure to recognize the purpose of listening. Four primary listening purposes exist.

- Appreciative listening
- Empathetic listening
- Comprehensive listening
- Critical listening

Six keys to improving listening have been offered in this chapter. These are:

- Listen ethically
- Use the entire listening process
- Delay evaluation
- Use thought speed effectively
- Minimize distractions
- Take effective notes

Key Terms

- appreciative listening
- emotion-laden words
- empathetic listening
- critical listening
- comprehensive listening
- listening
- attention
- attending
- comprehending
- remembering
- thought speed
- speech speed
- hearing

For Review and Discussion

1. Compare and contrast the four types of listening discussed in this chapter. Which do you think is the most important? Defend your answer.

2. Someone has suggested that there is a crisis of listening in America. Do you agree? Defend your answer.

3. Conduct your own study on the importance of listening by taking an eight-hour block of waking time and refusing to speak. Prepare a five to seven minute speech describing what you learned about communication in general and listening in particular as a result of the experience.

4. Keep a journal for an entire week of the times you failed to listen effectively. How would you evaluate your listening skills in light of this record? What were the results of listening failures? What could you do to improve?

Proclamation Practice

Prepare and deliver a two to three minute speech that demonstrates the importance of critical listening by analyzing the claims of a television commercial or print ad.

3

Speak Confidently

Chapter Challenges

A careful reading of Chapter 3 will provide insight into these chapter challenges:

1. How prevalent is the problem of communication apprehension or public speaking anxiety?
2. What are the five most common causes of public speaking anxiety?
3. Identify the "seven be's" that help to minimize the anxiety of public speaking.

At the Student Union Roundtable

"Where's Ryan?" Belsa asked as he eased into his seat at the student union roundtable. "All of the other members of the public speaking study group are here."

"Ryan's been here too" Jess answered with a grin. "In fact, he's been here and gone to the restroom twice in the twenty minutes since chapel. It appears that giving his speech next hour is having a serious impact on his bladder control."

"I know just how he feels." Cynthia laughed. "Last week when it was my turn to speak in class, I got so nervous that I didn't think I would get through it. In fact, I felt so sick that I thought I might be getting the flu."

"It was sweaty palms with me," Janelle said. "I kept dropping my pens and note cards as I put the finishing touches on my speech just before class. I've never been so nervous in all my life."

As Ryan returned to the table and greeted the discussion group members, Belsa added, "I don't recall having those physical symptoms when I gave my speech, but I just watched my video of the event. What a disaster! I was so nervous that I could not stand still. My roommate watched with me, and he claimed to have gotten seasick as a result of all that side to side rocking motion."

"It seems to affect us all in a different way," Jess concluded. "But no one seems to escape the anxiety. There must be some solution." He looked around the table at each participant hoping for a quick and easy solution.

Communication Anxiety: Widespread Problem

In a survey of Americans, the question was asked, "What are you most afraid of?" The number one response was "speaking before a group."[1] Since the fear of death ranked lower on the list, one might conclude that Americans would rather die than have to give a speech. Or as comedian Jerry Seinfeld noted, "This means to the average person, if you have to go to a funeral, you're better off in the casket than doing the eulogy."[2]

The fear of public speaking or *communication apprehension* is believed to be nearly universal. Prominent speakers—including politicians, industrialists, and pastors—have reported having communication anxiety or stage fright, sometimes called glossophobia.[3] Entertainers who have suf-

---

1. Wallechinsky, et al. *The Book of Lists*, 314.
2. Seinfeld, Sein *Language*, 120.
3. Storey, "*Communication Fears, Simple Fixes*," 104–106.

fered from overwhelming fear of public speaking include Babara Streisand, Carly Simon, and James Garner. Retired NBC weatherman Willard Scott is reportedly on the list. So too was the world-renowned cellist Pablo Casals.[4]

> *Communication apprehension*: Anxiety associated with standing before a group in order to give a speech.

When Georgia Democrat Zell Miller delivered the keynote address at the 2004 Republican National Convention, he was called many things, but timid was not among them. What few realized is how the firebrand public speaker first took to the rostrum. He remembers that it was in English class during his junior year of high school. He was selected to deliver one of six speeches in honor of George Washington's birthday. Miller describes the moment as a "knee-knocking experience" and declares, "I sweat bullets as I practiced and practiced."[5]

Miller's fellow Georgian and former First Lady Rosalynn Carter says she was forced to overcome the fear of public speaking in order to help her husband on the campaign trail. When describing her early speaking assignments, she uses words like "terrified" and "torture."[6]

In fact, it is even reported that Billy Graham, the most prominent evangelist of the late twentieth and early twenty-first centuries, suffered serious communication anxiety in his early efforts at public speaking.[7] One would hardly suspect Graham of being the victim of stage fright as he faithfully proclaimed the gospel to huge international audiences in later life.

Causes of Communication Anxiety

While the fact of communication anxiety is nearly universal, evidence indicates that the cause of the apprehension varies from one speaker to another. Five common reasons for communication anxiety prevail.

Fear of Failure

Often the anxiety over a current public speaking assignment grows as a result of a past performance problem. Many college students tell horror

---

4. Wilder, *7 Steps to Fearless Speaking*, 3.
5. Miller, *A National Party No More*, 141.
6. Carter, *The First Lady From Plains*, 69-71
7. Ackerman, *Great Souls*, 17.

stories about being humiliated by teachers or laughed at by peers in elementary school when they stood up before a group. Then, when they are forced to stand up in public later in life, that terrible day comes back to haunt them.

Of course, simply recalling a past failure does not produce communication apprehension all by itself. Instead the speaker projects those past failures onto future events and becomes consumed by the fear of future failure. The thought process may progress this way:

- In third grade I spoke up and was humiliated.
- I, therefore, associate speaking with humiliation.
- I assume that future speaking will lead to humiliation.

Sometimes the past failure is not even real. It can be projected onto the future public speaker by parents, teachers, or other adults who constantly berate a child as dull, stupid, or incapable. Repetition causes the child to believe the analysis and assume failure as the likely outcome for any new speech making venture. Extreme cases may require psychological counseling to break the pattern of anticipated failure.

Fear of Unknown

Another near-universal fear is the fear of the unknown. That prompts many to believe that a correlation exists between these two prominent fears. Instead of anticipating failure, the speaker may assume the outcome of a speech cannot be determined. Since there is no way to judge the end result of speaking, the act of speaking becomes a very frightening event. One student speaker reported, "I feel like I'm standing on the edge of a cliff and the assignment is to jump."

Perfectionism

High standards, lofty goals, and challenging aspirations are the hallmark of successful people. When these evolve into the need to be perfect, however, they can become debilitating. No speaker is perfect at public address. No speech accomplishes the speaker's intent perfectly. Speaking is about communicating, not about being perfect.[8]

One student speaker intended to drop the public speaking class after the first brief assignment. Her instructor had encouraged the class to avoid vocalized pauses like "uh" or "um" in the speech. When she used fillers

---

8. Wilder, *7 Steps to Fearless Speaking*, 12.

three times in a three-minute speech, her perfectionist tendencies led her to give up the challenge of learning public speaking.

Projection of Judgment

Another possibility is that the fear of public speaking exists because of the projection of a critical judge upon the audience. In this scenario perfectionist tendencies within a speaker are projected upon audience members. The speaker believes that the audience looks forward to the speaker's eventual failure. In reality the opposite is true. There is usually a high expectation of success within an audience. Those audiences that are made up of classmates especially want the speaker to succeed.

Preoccupation with Self

The fear of public speaking may also stem from an intense preoccupation with one's self. In the third and fourth chapters of Exodus, Moses demonstrates communication apprehension based on just such a preoccupation. In those chapters God calls Moses to go speak to Pharaoh on behalf of the people of Israel. Communication apprehension sets in, leading Moses to several attempts to change God's mind and negate God's call on his life. It is clear that Moses's real objection has to do with self-image, for in Exodus 4:10 he declares, "I have never been eloquent . . . . I am slow of speech and tongue" (NIV). But God calls Moses to a radical refocus by asking in Exodus 4:11, "Who gave man his mouth?"(NIV). Clearly, God is saying that one key to overcoming communication apprehension is to focus on God rather than on the self.

Such refocusing sets the stage for confident public speaking. It is interesting to note that the word confident comes from the Latin prefix con, meaning "with" and fideo, meaning "faith." Confident public speaking, then, is speaking with faith. It stems from recognition on the part of the speaker that he or she is not alone. In fact the speaker is not even the focus. For the Christian speaker, God is the focus. As a result, that speaker speaks confidently, or "with faith."

Reducing Communication Anxiety

Such refocusing from self to God goes a long way toward assisting the public speaker in reducing communication apprehension. But experts offer additional approaches to the problem. In fact, advice on minimizing communication apprehension is nearly as widespread as the problem itself. Some have suggested, for example, visualizing the audience with cabbage heads instead of human heads. Others say that imagining the audience members are all naked gives the speaker a sense of superiority and thus minimizes the anxiety. Such nonsense only serves to convince the beginning public speaker that there really is no solution for the problem aside from childish make-believe games.

So too, those who recommend drugs known as beta-blockers, which minimize the flow of adrenaline and thus reduce the feelings of anxiety, actually communicate defeat.[9] That is because they inadvertently teach that the problem of communication anxiety can not be naturally controlled.

On the other hand, there are some things the beginning public speaker can do to reduce the effects of communication anxiety. These are outlined below as the "Seven Be's" of anxiety reduction. It should be noted that using these "be's" will also improve overall speaking performance. In addition, careful adherence to the Seven Be's will invariably help to develop a speaker's communication confidence.

#1 Be Realistic

Syndicated columnist Kevin Cowherd satirically calls for a more realistic view of the potentials of public address when he answers the question "What is the worst that can happen?" While lighthearted, his words are indeed instructive. He writes, "Your mind goes blank and terror-stricken you lapse into a catatonic trance? The audience begins hooting and laughing at you? Startled from the trance by a tomato landing on your forehead, you flee the lectern in tears, only to rush home and lock yourself in a dark room for six months? Sure I guess all that could happen. Then again, it might not. You could be one of the lucky ones."[10]

Cowherd is pointing out that an objective and realistic appraisal of likely outcomes will usually serve to minimize the communication apprehension. Being realistic goes a long way in reducing the anxiety.

#2 Be Prepared

Since much communication apprehension is in reality fear of the unknown, the well-prepared speaker will usually experience less anxiety. Practicing the speech repeatedly leads to a lessening of anxiety that may accompany a search for just the right word. Many speakers report that repeated practice causes one word, phrase, or idea to trigger the next in their memory. As

---

9. Jacobs, "How To Relax in Public," 38.
10. Cowherd, "Speaking in Public no Scarier Than Flying."

a result, the content of the speech is familiar territory. Confidence grows with each trial run-through of the speech.

#3 Be Accepting

Ironically, one of the most important keys to reducing communication anxiety is to accept the reality of it. Some beginning speakers try to get the anxiety to go away. Those more experienced at public address, however, report the importance of relaxing and realizing that creative tension may even be positive for public speakers.

Athletes recognize that adrenaline can help create an excellent performance. One college basketball player noted, "The adrenaline rush before a big game can make my performance better than my skill-level." Communication apprehension also produces adrenaline. In the same way that adrenaline improves an athletic performance it can improve a speaker's performance as well.

#4 Be Fit

Many of the activities in which speakers engage because of communication apprehension actually intensify the problem. Marty actually passed out during the early moments of a speech of self-introduction in his public speaking class. Both Marty and his instructor initially blamed communication apprehension. Health professionals discovered, however, that Marty's blood-sugar level was dangerously low. He had failed to eat breakfast in order to rehearse his speech one final time. In addition, he was afraid the food would make his already nervous stomach even worse. Instead the lack of food led to the low-blood sugar problem.

In another public speaking class, Kelly experienced nearly uncontrollable shaking during her first speech. She revealed to her instructor that she had not slept the night before as a result of anxiety and the need to rehearse. Her instructor's advice to maintain a more normal schedule for the second speech yielded very favorable results. This was because Kelly's anxiety was better managed.

#5 Be Observant

Public speakers report in near universal numbers, that anxiety decreases as they observe their own abilities to perform in public speaking settings. Usually, public speaking instructors videotape speeches and require students to watch themselves on tape. After watching those videotaped performances, many students report that they actually performed better than they believed they did. Such realization builds confidence and reduces communication apprehension for subsequent speeches.

Molly was extremely nervous about giving her speech in class. After the delivery she declared, almost in tears, "I can't believe I did so poorly. I forgot everything I'd practiced. What a disaster!" Nothing Molly's instructor said could convince her that her performance was actually above average. Observing herself on videotape, however, accomplished the self-confidence transformation. "I had no idea I came across that well." Molly beamed. "I see some things to work on for sure, but it really was a good start."

#6 Be Expectant

A basic truth of life is that frequently we perform as we expect to perform. Nowhere is a *self-fulfilling prophecy* more likely to prove true than in the area of public speaking. That is why it is so important for a speaker to anticipate positive results from the speech. Those who expect to stumble over words and forget concepts often do precisely that. But the opposite is also true. Those who expect to perform well usually are very effective speakers. That is why some experts at dealing with communication apprehension recommend *performance visualization*.[11]

> *Self-fulfilling prophecy*: Process of anticipating certain outcomes and then behaving as if those outcomes already exist, thus creating as a reality what was anticipated.

In performance visualization, a speaker mentally pictures a successful speech in the short run. Over a longer period of time, the speaker builds upon several speaking successes and works toward developing a more positive attitude about public speaking. A positive self-perception as a speaker results from visualizing giving an effective speech. This positive visualization in turn becomes reality as the speaker's visual prophecy is self-fulfilled.

> *Performance visualization*: Process of mentally picturing a successful speech, thus creating a positive attitude and improved performance.

---

11. Ayers and Hopf, *Coping With Speech Anxiety*, 31–47.

While the technique may yield some positive results, the beginning speech student should remember that nothing positive is achieved without hard work. Simply imagining one's self as an effective speaker will not make it so. On the other hand, the hard work of careful research, masterful organization, and dedicated practice invariably will yield the desired results.

#7 Be Positive

Byron had a greater than average problem with communication apprehension. In spite of rigorous preparation, he became extremely agitated and thus less than effective in his speech deliveries. Byron characterized the problem by reporting, "I start out with a bit of the dry mouth, which causes me to stumble over a few words, which causes me to stutter because I know I'm messing up, which causes me to forget my next point . . . "

Byron's analysis is an accurate representation of the communication apprehension problem for many speakers. He has described a *regressive spiral* where anxiety creates a problem, which in turn creates more anxiety. Regressive spirals can be so devastating that one communication anxiety expert refers to them as panic spirals.[12]

A *progressive spiral* could solve Byron's problem. The progressive spiral could grow out of Byron's positive expectations about his performance. He expects to do well. He realizes the positive aspects of his performance, which create an even greater positive expectation.

> *Regressive spiral*: In communication apprehension a regressive spiral occurs when the anticipation of anxiety repeatedly creates more anxiety.
>
> *Progressive spiral*: Spiral that occurs when repeated positive expectations about a speech lead to a better speech.

The progressive spiral works not just within a particular speech, but for a lifetime of communication apprehension as well. Instead of focusing on the time in elementary school when she was laughed at, Brittany searched her memory bank for positive speaking experiences. In order to create a more positive attitude toward public speaking, she dwelt upon these experiences. Later, when Brittany stepped to the lectern to deliver

---

12. Wilder, *7 Steps To Fearless Speaking*, 14.

her first in-class speech her mind was filled with her past successes, however insignificant they might seem. She expected to succeed again. She spoke confidently. So can you!

The Chapter in Brief

Communication anxiety is a common problem that has affected even the most talented public speakers. The problem is rooted in one or more of five causes:

- Fear of failure
- Fear of the unknown
- Perfectionism
- Projection of judgment
- Preoccupation with self

Communication anxiety never totally goes away. It can be effectively channeled, however, by careful adherence to the Seven Be's of anxiety control.

- Be realistic
- Be prepared
- Be accepting
- Be fit
- Be observant
- Be expectant
- Be positive

Key Terms

- communication apprehension
- performance visualization
- regressive spiral
- progressive spiral
- fear of the unknown
- fear of failure
- self-fulfilling prophecy

For Review and Discussion

1. Divide a blank sheet of paper with a line from top to bottom. On the left side list all of those occasions when you have observed public speakers failing. Consider failure as being when the speakers

were ridiculed, humiliated, or became the object of scorn. On the right side list the times you have seen speakers accomplish their purpose and receive applause. What does comparing the two lists tell you about audience expectations, communication apprehension, and the likelihood of failure?

2. On a scale of one to ten (where one is complete calm, and ten is sheer panic), how would you rate your communication apprehension? How does your self-rating compare with those of your discussion group? How does the rating of others compare to their actual speaking performance?

3. Which of the causes for communication apprehension listed in this chapter is most likely the source of your personal public speaking anxiety? Why do you think that is true?

4. Should Christians have a different level of communication apprehension than non-believers? Explain your answer.

Proclamation Practice

Prepare a three to five minute speech on the topic "My Most Frightening Experience." As classmates' speeches are delivered notice how few relate to public speaking. Prepare to answer the question "How realistic is the fear of public speaking?"

4

Speaking Ethically

Chapter Challenges

A careful reading of Chapter 4 will provide insights into these chapter challenges:

1. What is ethics? How does one develop a personal ethic?
2. What are the most common ethical systems? How do these systems address moral questions?
3. Describe the basic responsibilities of an ethical public speaker.

At The Student Union Roundtable

There was an attitude of celebration as the public speaking study group gathered at the student union roundtable. Ryan had delivered his speech to persuade earlier in the day and the members of the group agreed that he had done a masterful job.

"What a super speech to persuade, Ryan," Belsa said as he slid into his seat at the roundtable. "You had them eating out of your hand."

"Thanks." Ryan grinned. "I'm just glad to have it over."

Jannelle continued the spontaneous evaluation. "I thought it was very well done. Monroe's Motivated Sequence was clear and powerful. I think you persuaded a lot of our classmates to be more open and tolerant toward other cultures."

Ryan looked a bit sheepish. "I hope I didn't do too good a job of convincing them."

"How could you be too convincing?" Cynthia asked. "After all, it is a speech to persuade."

"Well," Ryan said, "my thesis statement was, 'In this speech I will convince the audience that it makes no difference what culture or heritage or religion you are from, since we are all God's children.' But I actually don't believe that."

"You don't?" Jannelle gasped. "It sounds right to me, and you were very persuasive."

"Of course I don't believe that. I am a follower of the one who said, 'I am *the* way, *the* truth, and *the* life, no one comes to the Father but by me.' Jesus obviously believed it made a difference what religion one followed. And September 11 helped to confirm that for me."

"So why did you take the opposite position in your speech?" asked Jess.

"It started out as an attempt at satire." Ryan defended himself. "I guess I got a little bit carried away. I ended up persuading the audience of something I don't believe at all."

"I feel like I've been had," said Belsa dejectedly. "I'm not sure you should have done that."

Ethical Questions

The roundtable discussion is about to enter the important world of *ethics* and public speaking. The study of ethics grows out of general philosophical and moral beliefs about how people treat one another. Ethics is the system of moral standards used to determine right and wrong.

> *Ethics*: System of moral standards used to determine right and wrong.

Most people have no difficulty discussing ethics or moral choices as they relate to social questions such as abortion or gun control. While they might not agree on the answers to the questions, they recognize that those issues do have moral implications. It is sometimes more difficult, however, to identify the moral implications associated with choices relative to public speaking. Never the less, these implications are very real. In fact, every decision has an ethical aspect. That includes decisions about public speaking. When Ryan decided to adopt a thesis statement contrary to his personal viewpoint, he made a choice with moral dimensions.

Sue Ellen also made a decision with moral and therefore ethical dimensions. She borrowed major portions of her speech to inform from her fiancée who had taken the same public speaking course a few semesters earlier. Sue Ellen made a decision about the use of time without giving much thought to ethics.

Chris implied in his speech to inform on the topic of investment strategy that he was heavily invested in mutual funds. In reality it was Chris's mother, a licensed investment broker who owned the investments and shared information with Chris. Chris made a decision about developing his credibility in the speech. That decision of course had ethical and moral dimensions.

Ethical Systems

As different speakers wrestle with the moral decisions associated with speech development and delivery, they often reach far different conclusions about the propriety of certain actions. As we have seen, Ryan concluded that it was acceptable to convince his audience of a position with which he himself did not agree. Belsa holds the opposite point of view.

One of the reasons that all speakers do not arrive at the same decision with regard to moral questions is that all speakers do not use the same ethical system to evaluate the questions. A brief review of six of the most popular ethical systems is in order.[1]

---

1. For a more comprehensive discussion of ethical systems see Rae, *Moral Choices*; Van Wyk, *An Introduction to Ethics*; or Hosmer, *The Ethics of Management*.

Ethical Egoism

Ethical egoism asserts that the morality of an act is determined by personal self-interest. In this system, actions promoting self-interest are moral. And, conversely, those actions that do not promote self-interest are not moral.

In spite of the fact that the system appears on the surface to be extremely narcissistic, Scott Rae notes that ethical egoism is used in the Bible to motivate people to be obedient to God.[2] In Deuteronomy 27–30 for example, obedience is encouraged because it leads to the rewards of prosperity and peace.

Chad's public speaking instructor assigned a speech on gun control. The assignment included that the speech must be a speech to persuade, but the exact position on that topic was up to the speaker. Chad and his classmates could take any position, from the complete banning of all weapons for private citizens to no restrictions whatsoever on the right to keep and bear arms. Chad knew that his instructor was a strong supporter of the Second Amendment and a member of the National Rifle Association. Chad chose to support only very limited gun control in his speech. He reasoned, "I really could not care less about the topic. So I may as well try to impress Dr. Hobbs with my position." Chad made the decision about his speech topic on the basis of ethical egoism.

Utilitarianism

A second ethical system is called *utilitarianism*. According to this system that which produces the most good, or the least harm, for the most people is the ethical choice. The utilitarian system is sometimes referred to as consequentialism because decisions are primarily based on the consequences of an action. The term teleological, with its prefix *teleo* meaning "end "or "goal," is also often applied to utilitarianism because this ethical system focuses on the end results of a particular action.

Dewayne had nearly completed his speech to inform on vitamin C. He had focused on the value of taking vitamin C supplements in order to avoid the common cold. Late in his preparation process, Dewayne discovered an article that suggested that taking too much of the vitamin could produce uncomfortable and harmful side effects. Dewayne decided to leave this information out of his speech. "The positive effect of vitamin C far outweighs any potential negatives," he reasoned. Dewayne made the decision within a utilitarian ethical system.

---

2. Rae, *Moral Choices*, 84.

Relativism

A third ethical system, *relativism*, teaches that no absolute moral truth exists and therefore no universal right and wrong. According to relativism, what is right in one situation or for one person may not necessarily be right for another person or in another situation. There are varying degrees of relativistic thinking in our culture today.

Joseph Fletcher popularized the relativistic system with his book *Situation Ethics*. He suggests that all morality is relative and that the right thing is the most loving thing in a particular situation. In relativism there is no such thing as absolute truth or an action that is absolutely right in every situation. The one exception seems to be that relativism is absolutely correct every time according to the proponents of this position.

Marge had a speech to persuade due for class on Monday. Over the weekend her roommate, who had been experiencing serious health problems, was taken to the hospital. She pleaded with Marge to stay with her until her family arrived from a neighboring state. Very late on Sunday evening, Marge returned to her dorm and borrowed a speech from an upper classman. Marge felt that her behavior was totally justified under the circumstances, since she had given her weekend preparation time to her roommate as an act of compassion and love. Marge used relativism in this instance of decision making.

Kantian Ethics

Yet another system for making decisions with moral implications has been developed by Immanuel Kant.[3] Kant's system is based upon two principles called "categorical imperatives."

- Act only on principles that you would be willing to make a universal law.
- Never treat yourself or other people as simply a means but also as an end.

Kant, using these two imperatives, offers a system that is built upon obligations and duties. He offers a consistent moral framework that recognizes the fact of right and wrong.

In peer evaluations Josh got very low marks on his speech to inform. He spent the five to seven minute speech teaching the class about various techniques for picking the nose. Some classmates were disgusted with the topic. Others saw the speech as a total waste of time. Many were uncon-

---

3. Kant, *Groundwork of the Metaphysics of Morals*.

sciously evaluating Josh on the basis of *Kantian ethics*. They were saying, in effect, "We would not want all of the speeches we hear to be so disgusting or trivial. We do not wish to have our time so wasted."

Absolutism

Some people make moral decisions on the basis of *absolutism*. This is the belief that there are absolute moral principles of right and wrong from which a decision-maker may never deviate. The absolutists do not allow for any exceptions no matter what the circumstances.

Some see absolutism and relativism as opposite ends of a continuum.[4] On the other hand, most decision-makers decide on right and wrong with rules existing somewhere between unchanging absolutes and circumstantial variations.

The Old Testament law tends toward the absolute end of that continuum. There is little deviation throughout the Old Testament from the principles of justice, equality, holiness, and integrity. However, in some cases absolutism can be narrow, rigid, and even harsh.

Paul took public speaking at a Christian liberal arts school. He had grown up in a home where dating was forbidden. Instead, his family used the term "courting" to describe the process of winning a future mate's heart. When Paul's speech instructor assigned a speech to inform on the topic "Describe Your Ideal Date" Paul became offended. He not only refused to complete the assignment, but instead of accepting his instructor's offer to negotiate the assignment, he dropped the class. Clearly, Paul's ethical system included a form of absolutism.

New Testament Ethics

The difference between the Old Testament absolutes and *New Testament ethics* is one of degrees not kind. Added to the absolutes of justice, equality, holiness, and integrity is a new emphasis on love. Jesus encapsulated that emphasis in what is called the golden rule. "Do to others what you would have them do to you."[5]

John Maxwell argues for an integration of the golden rule into every area of life.[6] He maintains that such an approach yields an avoidance of the compartmentalization that derives from having a business ethic, a family ethic, a church ethic, and a personal ethic.

---

4. Rae, *Moral Choices,* 93.
5. Matthew 7:12, New International Version
6. Maxwell, *There's No Such Thing as Business Ethics.*

The same argument can be applied to public speaking. There is no such thing as a public speaking ethic. Instead there are ethical people who do public speaking. And sadly, there are unethical people who speak publicly as well.

Responsibilities of Ethical Speakers

The concept of one ethical principle applied throughout life is especially true for the Christian public speaker. Those who have consecrated themselves to the Lordship of Jesus Christ will want to honor Him in every aspect of life. That, of course, includes the way that they prepare and deliver a speech. For the public speaker, honoring Christ means carefully considering five responsibilities of ethical public address.

Responsibility #1 Tell the Truth

Most public speaking ethicists agree with the position articulated by Solomon in Proverbs 16:13. He wrote, "Kings take pleasure in honest lips; they value a man who speaks the truth" (NIV). Telling the truth is a basic of public speaking ethics.

In a speech on dog obedience training, Josh said that he had trained his own and several other animals. Josh made the statement in order to increase his credibility on the subject. In fact, he had never trained a dog but had read several books on the subject and had watched a "how to" video. When challenged, Josh admitted that he had "stretched the truth." "I could do it," he said. "I just never have." Josh's statement in the speech was unethical. It violated the first responsibility of ethical public speakers, which is to tell the truth.

In addition to avoiding the kind of blatant lies that Josh told, the ethical public speaker should also take care to eliminate any *false impressions*. False impressions are true statements that are designed to conjure up for the audience an image that is not accurate.

> *False impressions*: True statements designed to conjure up for the audience an image that is not accurate.

For example, Eric said, in his speech on the importance of voting, "I have never missed a presidential election since I became eligible to vote." In reality Eric's age meant he had only been eligible for one such election. He had in fact failed to vote in two off-year elections since becoming eligible and had never participated in a primary. Eric's statement was factual, but of questionable ethics since it left a false impression of strong civic mindedness.

In a speech of self-introduction, Ethan declared, "My family comes from a long line of hearty rugged Scandinavian stock." Ethan's last name, Sorenson, added to the impression that he was of Norwegian descent. In reality, Ethan's ancestry was mixed and had been diluted through inter-ethnic marriage. Since he had traced the family tree, Ethan knew that he was only 1/32 Norwegian. Ethan intentionally left an unethical false impression.

In addition to outright falsehoods and false impressions, the ethical public speaker will avoid the use of *partial truths*. Partial truths involve leaving out some strategic facts that, if known by the members of the audience, would likely change their conclusion.

> *Partial truths*: Leaving out some strategic facts that if known by the audience, may change their likely conclusion.

Calvin used a partial truth in his speech to inform when he said, "Not one pastor in my denomination has ever been convicted of embezzling church funds." Calvin went on to make a point of the integrity of leadership within the small denomination to which he belonged. What Calvin failed to say, however, was that three pastors, while not yet convicted, were currently facing formal charges. That constituted a significant percentage in his small denomination. In addition, five non-pastoral church leaders had been convicted of those precise charges in just the last three years. Calvin's use of a partial truth was unethical.

Paula used a partial truth in her speech to persuade on gun control when she declared, "According to my class survey only one in twenty from this class currently has a firearm." In fact, Paula's survey asked whether the respondent had a firearm with them on campus. Since campus regulations prohibited firearms on university property, the one respondent either was violating the rules or misunderstood the question. Further, Paula knew from the survey that nearly 50 percent of the class owned a firearm which they kept at home or in another safe off-campus location. That data, however, did not support Paula's contention that the Second Amendment should be repealed. Therefore she unethically chose to tell a partial truth.

Ethical public speakers tell the truth, the whole truth, and nothing but the truth from the public speaking lectern just as they would under oath in a court of law. In addition to not lying, they do not steal as noted in Responsibility #2.

Responsibility #2 Give Proper Credit

Speakers who present another person's words or ideas as their own without giving proper credit are guilty of *plagiarism*. The word plagiarism has a Latin root identical to the word for kidnap. That implies that to use someone's words or ideas without credit is to kidnap those words or ideas. Such behavior is unethical. Sadly about 40 percent of students admit to plagiarism at least once during the past year.[7] An increasing number of these students use the Internet in order to plagiarize. The abundance of services that write papers or speeches for a fee is testimony to the growing market. Regardless of where the material comes from, however, passing off someone else's words or ideas as one's own is plagiarism, a form of stealing, and a moral and ethical wrong.

> *Plagiarism*: Presenting another person's words or ideas as one's own without giving proper credit.

Angela found herself pressed for the time she needed to prepare her speech to persuade. She was a pledge to a campus sorority, which kept a file of coursework completed by members in previous semesters. Angela "checked out" a speech by a sorority sister and delivered the speech as her own work. Angela is guilty of plagiarism and according to the ethos of most colleges and universities will, when caught, receive a penalty ranging from failure in the assignment to dismissal from school.[8]

Angela's infraction is sometimes referred to as *global plagiarism*.[9] That is the plagiarism that results from using an entire speech that has been written by another. Instead Scott engaged in *patchwork plagiarism*.[10] His speech was not the work of one other author, but pieces from a speech, an encyclopedia article, and his roommate's term paper. He cut and pasted

---

7. Finkel, "Sticky Fingers on The Information Superhighway," 6–9.
8. Roberts, "Plagiarism," 11.
9. Lucas, *The Art of Public Speaking*, 43.
10. Ibid., 44.

the three works together to create a speech. Only the transitions originated with Scott.

> *Global plagiarism*: Using an entire speech that has been written by another.
>
> *Patchwork plagiarism*: Patching together large segments of speeches that have been written by others.

Katy's ethical infraction was not quite as broad as Angela's and Scott's, but it was just as serious. In a speech where she proposed her opinion that Ronald Reagan was the greatest president ever to hold office, she described his first inauguration: "It was overcast. But as Reagan took his place behind the podium and looked at the chief justice of the Supreme Court, the sun burst through the clouds in what he remembered as 'an explosion of warmth and light.' He could feel the heat on his face as he recited the oath of office. His left hand was on his mother's Bible, which was open to II Chronicles 7:14." Katy failed to mention that those were the words of Peggy Noonan from her biography of the former president.[11]

In order to use the same words in an ethical manner, Katy might have prefaced them by saying, "Reagan biographer Peggy Noonan reported . . . " It would not be necessary for Angela to give the complete bibliographic information in her speech. She does, however, need to use a *verbal citation* in order to tell the audience who is responsible for the words. A verbal citation gives the audience enough information as a part of the speech so that they can find the source if they so desire.

> *Verbal citation*: Giving credit in a speech by providing enough information so that an audience member can find the source if they so desire.

Since Katy's motivations are not known, it is impossible to determine whether she is guilty of *intentional plagiarism* or *unintentional plagiarism*. Unintentional plagiarism is sometimes the result of sloppy research or careless note taking. It is, however, just as serious as intentional plagiarism and may, in spite of intent, have legal as well as ethical ramifications for the speaker.

---

11. Noonan, *When Character Was King*, 160.

> *Intentional plagiarism*: Consciously using the words or work of another as if they were one's own.
>
> *Unintentional plagiarism*: Unconsciously using the words of another in a speech as a result of sloppy research or careless notetaking.

Responsibility #3 Respect the Audience

In a demonstration speech to inform, Alan selected as his topic "How to Start a Car." Alan dramatically demonstrated the proper procedure for inserting and turning the key, as well as when to end the twisting motion. Alan spoke truthfully, yet the topic was viewed by many of his colleagues as so common-sense and trivial as to be inappropriate. Many even argued on their peer evaluation forms that Alan had wasted their time. According to one analysis, since twenty-four classmates each gave Alan seven minutes of their time, a total of 168 minutes, or nearly three hours of productive time was wasted in the endeavor. Such disrespect for the audience is unethical.

Ironically, in the same public speaking class and on the same assignment Kelly also gave a speech relating to automobiles. She demonstrated how to drive a car with a stick shift transmission. That was a skill that her father had taught her and that only about 50 percent of the class had developed. While some in the class had already mastered the stick shift, all of the students in her audience found Kelly's speech interesting and informative. When asked about the contrasting reactions, they argued that the difference was that Kelly did not talk down to her audience as Alan had. She respected their intelligence.

Respecting the audience includes respecting their point of view as well as their time. In a speech to persuade on capital punishment, Scott acknowledged those who believe in the Old Testament principle of an eye for an eye and a tooth for a tooth, but he referred to people who hold that belief as "hedonistic barbarians." Scott's slam on several members of his audience was of highly questionable ethics. Ethical speakers can feel passionate about their position and can hold their point of view strongly, but they must also respect their audience.

Respect for the audience also encompasses the concept of civility. Civility is behavior that is civilized and is marked by politeness, consideration, and courtesy. It is behavior that respects the rights and dignity of others even while disagreeing with them.[12] Civil speakers do not resort to name calling or other derogatory language. They graciously accept the listener's right to reject the speaker's position.

Responsibility #4 Balance the Appeals

The fourth responsibility of an ethical public speaker is the responsibility to balance emotional and rational appeals. Questions about this principle arise most frequently in the development of a speech to persuade.

Both Aaron and Samantha delivered their speeches to persuade in an attempt to get classmates to sponsor an overseas child through World Vision or some other charitable organization. Aaron used strictly an emotional appeal. He showed pictures and told stories of starving, broken, emaciated children. Samantha, on the other hand, used some of the same emotional appeals to present her case. She also used rational appeals, however, suggesting ways her classmates could join together to help meet the need. She presented data about the affluence of Americans as compared to that of people in other parts of the world. She gave examples of how friends on other campuses had begun sponsoring a child. Peer evaluators gave Samantha higher marks than Aaron. They reported feeling more challenged to make a good decision by Samantha's approach. Aaron's strictly emotional appeal left them feeling used. According to the audience's reports, it seemed as if he did not trust them to analyze the facts and make a good decision.

Responsibility #5 Consider the Effects

Troy attended a Christian university that forbids dancing. Troy believed that prohibition was unnecessary and grossly out of date. In his speech to persuade, Troy attempted to convince his class that the rule should be abolished. His call to action invited the class to join him at a "dance-in" on the campus commons on Saturday night. The event was to protest the no-dance policy. Administrators, however, reacted with unexpected harshness to the protest event. Fifteen students received expulsions from the university for their involvement. Lesser penalties affected a larger number of students. The group receiving the most serious discipline included Troy and two of his classmates, who had responded to his speech. While he continued to disagree with the rule, Troy realized after the fact that he had not carefully considered the effect of his speech. He regretted his audience's

---

12. Hamilton, "A Responsibility For Civility," 19.

members' expulsion. But by then it was too late for Troy to reconsider the impact of his speech.

Of course, the impact of a speech will not always be positive. It must, however, be carefully considered in advance of delivery. Leah convinced two of her audience-member classmates to participate with her in a protest against abortion in her college town. The trio was arrested for their involvement and also experienced discipline at school for the incident. Leah had carefully calculated the possible outcomes, however, in advance of giving the speech. In spite of the results, Leah and her colleagues believed she acted ethically because she had considered the potential effect of her speech.

The Chapter in Brief

As in every area of life, ethical questions sometimes arise during speech development and delivery. As a result, it is important for the speaker to understand the basics of the most common ethical systems. These include:

- Ethical Egoism
- Utilitarianism
- Relativism
- Kantian Ethics
- Absolutism
- New Testament Ethics

Honoring Jesus Christ in all of life's activities is the ethic of a Christian. For the Christian public speaker, that ethic plays out in five important responsibilities. These five are the minimum ethical standards. They are:

- Tell the truth
- Give proper credit
- Respect the audience
- Balance appeals
- Consider effects

Key Terms

Use the list below to test your knowledge of the vocabulary introduced in this chapter.

- ethics
- ethical egoism
- relativism

- Kantian ethics
- absolutism
- verbal citation
- utilitarianism
- New Testament ethics
- global plagiarism
- patchwork plagiarism
- false impressions
- partial truths
- plagiarism
- intentional plagiarism
- unintentional plagiarism

For Review and Discussion

1. Ryan revealed that he persuaded his audience of a position he did not agree with in the roundtable discussion at the beginning of the chapter. Has Ryan behaved ethically? Answer the question six times by using each of the six systems outlined in this chapter. With which opinion do you agree? Why?

2. Earlier we saw that Chad took a position for his speech to persuade on gun control in the hopes of impressing his instructor, Dr. Hobbs. Chad really did not hold to his stated position or, for that matter, to any position. Did Chad behave ethically in your opinion? Which ethical systems would lead to answers that agree with yours? Which would yield contrary results?

3. The discussion of ethics presented in this chapter focuses on the ethical responsibility of the speaker. But the audience has ethical responsibilities as well. List some of the ethical responsibilities of an audience.

Proclamation Practice

Choose a controversial social issue such as euthanasia, universal health care, Medicare reform, civil unions, or abortion. Prepare a three to five minute speech discussing the ethical issues involved in the national debate.

5

Deciding on a Speech Topic

Chapter Challenges

A careful reading of Chapter 5 will provide insight into these chapter challenges:

1. What are some of the ways to generate preliminary speech topics?
2. Define brainstorming. How does brainstorming impact the selection of a speech topic?
3. A preliminary speech topic should be matched to what three important considerations?
4. What is audience analysis? Why is it important to the public speaker?
5. Describe the difference between a speech type, a speech topic, and a speech thesis.
6. List the characteristics of an effective thesis statement.

At the Student Union Roundtable

There were lots of long faces at the student union roundtable as the public speaking study group took their places. "I can't believe we're all in the same boat," said Ryan. "Not one of us with a topic for a speech that is due in less than a week."

"We've been so busy with tests and papers that we've waited way too long," moaned Belsa.

"But time is now short. This is a definite priority. What are we going to do?" Janelle laid her head on the table.

"Get a grip," said Cynthia. "First, let's make sure we understand the assignment."

Jess read from his public speaking notebook, "The assignment is to deliver a three to five minute speech that completes the sentence, 'I believe the greatest American ever is _____.'"

"Clearly, what we need is a speech of celebration," said Ryan.

Belsa responded. "Correct. But, that is not the problem. The assignment is so wide open that we could use anybody."

"Politicians," offered Cynthia.

"Entertainers," continued Janelle.

"Sport's figures," added Ryan.

"Personal friends," said Jess.

"Or relatives," Belsa joined in.

"I hadn't thought of some of those categories," admitted Cynthia. "Believe it or not, this conversation has already helped. I have a couple of ideas."

"Me too," Janelle said. "Let's make a list together under each of those categories. Start with the politicians and everyone just call out names. I'll record them for us."

Type, Topic, or Thesis

Cynthia's call to "make sure we understand the assignment" proved critical in getting the student union roundtable group started correctly. Often speakers begin the process of topic selection unsure of how to even define the term *topic*. In fact, three important pieces of information must be clear to the speaker at this early stage of speech development. These include type, topic, and thesis. These constitute the three *T's* of speech preparation.

Type

Every speech has a purpose. That purpose is the speech *type*. Speeches generally fit into one of four types:

- Speeches to inform
- Speeches to persuade
- Speeches to edify
- Speeches to celebrate

Speeches to inform are designed to teach the audience something that the speaker believes they will find interesting or beneficial. The dissemination of information, not the alteration of opinion, is the primary purpose of such a speech.

In a speech to persuade, the speaker hopes to change the attitudes, beliefs, or values of audience members. Usually, as a result of persuasion, there is also an accompanying change in behavior on the part of respondents. The speech to persuade always has a clear call to action.

Speeches to edify are used primarily by the Christian community since such speeches are designed to build up the church. Edification speeches generally take the form of a testimony, an expository lesson, or a faith lesson.

Finally, speeches to celebrate encompass a whole host of speech forms. Welcome speeches, introductions, eulogies, acceptance speeches, and nominations all fit into this general type.

With an invitation to speak there often comes information as to the type of speech required. For example, often the instructor of a public speaking class will assign one of the four types and allow the student to choose a topic. When the type of speech expected from any public speaking opportunity is not clearly spelled out, the effective speaker clarifies that important piece of information early.

Topic

The term *topic* is used to indicate the broad subject matter that the speech will cover. Selection of a topic is only the first step in the process of declaring the precise statement of what the speaker hopes to accomplish in the speech. A topic is a very broad beginning and must eventually be narrowed.

As an avid golfer and member of the university intercollegiate golf team, Seth knew as soon as he heard the assignment for a speech to inform that he wanted to do his speech on golf. Seth had already decided on a speech topic. The determination of that topic, of course, eliminated thousands of potential speeches. Seth was not going to speak on basketball, football, or volleyball. He also had eliminated career selection, house painting, or music appreciation. But Seth's topic remained very broad. Whether he would discuss the history of golf, the procedure for playing, the rules of the game, or course selection still had to be determined.

Thesis

Once the topic has been sufficiently narrowed, the effective speaker will write a thesis statement. The *thesis statement* is a one-sentence statement of what the speaker intends to accomplish in the speech. It should be written as a statement, not a question, and should use precise descriptive language.

> *Thesis statement*: One sentence statement of what the speaker hopes to accomplish in the speech.

After carefully considering available research, his own interests, and what he believed were the interests and needs of the audience, Seth decided on a thesis statement. "This speech will inform the audience about the five best golf courses in our state," he wrote. Seth had now determined the speech thesis in addition to the type (informative) and the topic (golf).

Generating Preliminary Topics

Deciding on a topic and narrowing it down to a specific thesis statement is sometimes as difficult as actually giving the speech. The first step involves considering preliminary topics. These preliminary topics may be generated through several means.

Brainstorming

In order to discover names for the greatest American speech, the round-table discussion group used a modified form of *brainstorming*. Groups that brainstorm for ideas usually set a specific time frame in which to work. Everyone suggests possible topics, while one person records all of these topic ideas. According to the rules of brainstorming, there are no off-limits topics or statements. Of course, later refinement will undoubtedly be necessary, but in the beginning generating ideas is the key. Sometimes groups go around the table with each participant taking a turn in order. Some believe, however, that those groups where there is no conversational control are more productive.[1] Everyone simply offers ideas as they come to mind regardless of whose turn it is perceived to be. Brainstorming done properly is demanding and hard work, but it produces a plethora of ideas.[2]

Preliminary Research

A second means of generating speech topics involves doing preliminary research. Scanning a magazine or journal often yields topic ideas. Textbooks for courses beyond public speaking can prove a very rich mine of topic ideas—so too can using an Internet search engine such as Yahoo or Google.

That was the approach Janelle used. After the roundtable meeting broke up she went to the library and put the topic "great Americans" into Google. That preliminary search yielded more than nineteen million hits and provided scores of possible names for her speech. Just from the names offered on one of the hits about the Great American Museum located at Bronx Community College in New York, she added the names of Alexander Graham Bell, Eli Whitney, George Westinghouse, Daniel Chester French, and James Earl Fraser to her list of potential topics.

Current Events

Belsa also went to the library after the roundtable discussion. Instead of getting online, however, he went to the newspaper racks to check on the day's news. While reading about the events of the day, he began to notice the names that were prominent in the stories. From just one page dedicated to world and national news in the local small-town newspaper, he added George W. Bush, Michael Jackson, General Norman Swartzkoff, and Condoleezza Rice to his list of potential speech topics.

For other speech topics databases such as those available for most major newspapers may prove helpful. The wire services for many newspapers, including The Associated Press and Reuters, can also be accessed online. When topics are important enough to be covered in the news, the speaker will usually have little difficulty finding sufficient information later in the speech development process.

---

1. Nijstad et al., "Production Blocking and Idea Generation," 531–49.
2. Colwell, "Brainstorming," 9–13.

Preselected Topics

Sometimes the audience requests a topic. For example, sometimes a speaker is asked to speak on a specific topic or for a specific occasion. The invitation has therefore already limited the topic. Speakers report that these assigned topics are sometimes more difficult to develop because they are outside the speaker's passion and interest. This leads to the practice of *reframing alternatives*. When a speaker reframes alternatives, he or she alters the topic slightly from what was assigned by the audience members or their representative.

> *Reframing the alternatives:* Act of altering a topic slightly from what was assigned by the audience members or their representative.

Joy attended a small denominational college. The youth pastor of her church invited Joy to speak to the senior high students on the topic "The Advantages of Choosing a Denominational School." While Joy was basically happy with her college, she also knew there were some downsides. Her speech, with permission of the inviting pastor, became "The Advantages and Disadvantages of Choosing a Denominational School." Joy had reframed the alternatives but still used the preliminary topic assigned by her audience representative.

Audience Needs

On other occasions the audience may allow the speaker to choose a subject, but the interests or needs of the audience suggest topics. "Planning for Retirement Early" may be an excellent speech to inform for a college public speaking class. On the other hand, "Surviving on Social Security" is not relevant to that particular audience. In general, their interests simply do not match that topic.

Perceived audience needs may sometimes suggest a topic. For example, Belsa choose Arnold Schwarzenegger for his great American speech. An audience need, noted by Belsa, helped him select that topic. As a Honduran citizen studying in the United States, he believed his class would benefit from exposure to the contributions of foreign born citizens. The Austrian-born governor of California became a subject that helped Belsa meet that audience need.

Speaker Interests

One of the most significant sources of preliminary topics stems from the interests of the speaker. It is simply easier and more fun for a speaker to talk about things of personal interest. Such interests sometimes include hobbies, favorite courses, favorite activities, part-time jobs, career interests, or favorite vacation spots.

Amanda was stumped for a topic for her speech to inform. As the deadline loomed, she asked her instructor, Dr. Conley, for help. "Where are you from again?" asked Dr. Conley.

"Van Buren, Indiana," answered Amanda proudly. "But I fail to see how that can help."

"Is there nothing interesting or unique about Van Buren?" Dr. Conley quizzed.

"Well," Amanda responded tentatively, "Van Buren is the popcorn capital of the world."

As a result of that discussion, Amanda began to think preliminarily of a topic relating to Van Buren, the popcorn capital. Ultimately, her speech to inform, "A Small Town with a Big Difference," was interesting to the entire class. Part of her success was that the preliminary topic sprang from Amanda's personal interests.

Jess's great American speech provides an additional example. He was very interested in all areas of athletics but most especially in baseball. In order to generate some preliminary topics, Jess composed a list of baseball greats who might also be considered great Americans. From that list it was a simple matter to narrow his topic to the legendary Jackie Robinson.

Narrowing the Topic

In addition to providing a great source of preliminary topics, speaker interests serve to begin the process of narrowing the topic. It is, therefore, the first of three important matching exercises through which the effective speaker will pass a preliminary topic.

Matching the Topic to the Speaker

For a given speaker the universal list of all possible topics can be categorized into just three lists.

1. Topics the speaker knows about.
2. Topics the speaker would like to know about.
3. Topics about which the speaker has no knowledge or interest.

Generally, it is wise to avoid the third category when possible. On the other hand, matching the topic to the speaker may involve either of the other two. Good speech topics often flow from the speaker's knowledge or the speaker's interests.

Susan had already earned an associate degree in medical record-keeping when she decided to finish her bachelor's degree at a Bible College. Her speech to inform grew out of her knowledge and past experience. She spoke on the modern equivalent to several prominent Bible diseases. The research for Susan was not nearly as extensive as it would have been for other students in the class.

While speaker understanding is important to the topic selection process, it is not the only important aspect. Prior knowledge is seldom sufficient to produce an excellent written composition.[3] The same could be said of the production of a speech.

Carmen's speech to inform grew more out of her interests than her knowledge. She felt certain that God had called her to missions. She was earning a degree in preparation for response to that call. Carmen's speech on people groups who have no New Testament translation was a tremendous challenge to her in terms of doing the research. She was willing to research, however, because of her extraordinary interest in the subject.

Matching the Topic to the Audience

In addition to matching the preliminary topic to the speaker's interest, it is essential to match the topic to the audience. The process of discovering an audience's makeup and interests is called *audience analysis*.[4] The effective public speaker always does audience analysis prior to the development of the speech. In the process of that analysis, the speaker searches for at least three types of information.

> *Audience analysis*: Process by which a speaker discovers an audience's makeup and interests.

Demographic audience analysis includes information such as the gender or age of the audience members. The socio-economic status of the audience members is another piece of demographic information that may be important to the topic development. In addition, the speaker may need

---

3. McKenna and McKenna, "Selecting Topics for Research Writing," 53–59.
4. Callison and Lamb, "Audience Analysis," 34–40.

to know something about the audience members' religions, group affiliations, or racial and ethnic backgrounds.

> *Demographic audience analysis*: Process of discovering information such as the gender, age, socioeconomic status, religion, race, or ethnicity of audience members.

Misty had been born into an upper middle-class family where both of her parents were highly paid professionals. In a speech to persuade, "Dismantling the Welfare State," Misty referred to government-sponsored student loans as "a giant handout program for those who won't work." Misty's lack of sensitivity would be problematic in any audience. In a class where 97 percent of the students received such assistance, her statement was inexcusable. The problem arose because she failed to do demographic audience analysis.

In addition to demographic audience analysis, the effective speaker will perform a *psychological audience analysis*. Psychological audience analysis seeks to discover the beliefs, values, and attitudes of an audience in relation to the topic of the speech. In addition, it considers the audience's predisposition to the speaker and to the topic.

> *Psychological audience analysis*: Seeks to discover the beliefs, values, and attitudes of an audience relative to the topic of the speech.

Alan was the only Jewish student on a predominately evangelical Christian campus. His speech to inform, "The Jesus Myth," was designed to explain why he was convinced that Jesus could not be the Messiah. He realized that he had selected a topic with an enormous challenge. That challenge was greatly enhanced, however, when he said, "Christians have been lied to and have insisted on lying to others." Less inflammatory language could have accomplished Alan's purpose. He failed to recognize that calling his classmates liars would incite an extremely negative reaction because he failed to adequately accomplish a psychological audience analysis.

Finally, complete audience analysis will usually need to include an aspect known as *situational audience analysis*. Here the speaker analyzes elements such as the size of the audience and the physical setting in which the speech will take place.

> *Situational audience analysis*: Considers the size of the audience and the physical setting where the speech will take place.

In her speech to inform, Jennifer planned to use a question and answer period near the end of the speech. She visualized the speech being given in her public speaking lab section of twenty-four students. She failed to realize that her speech was scheduled for the day usually devoted to the weekly lecture. That meant that six lab sections were combined for a total audience of nearly one hundred and fifty. Jennifer recognized too late that the audience size made the question and answer format nearly unmanageable. She wished later that she had done a better job of situational audience analysis.

Tyrone planned to use a PowerPoint presentation for his speech. He practiced the speech on the PC in his dorm room. The classroom computer, however, refused to read Tyrone's CD. The result was a disastrous presentation in which Tyrone attempted to present a PowerPoint presentation without the graphics. For Tyrone, situational audience analysis would have meant testing the compatibility of his disc with the classroom computer.

Sometimes audience analysis is as simple as testing a disc in a computer a few days before the speech delivery. In other cases, more sophisticated means of data collection are required to accomplish effective audience analysis. For example, questionnaires are a common tool for audience analysis information gathering.

Before Brett gave his speech to persuade on capital punishment, he surveyed the class audience on their current beliefs. Brett used yes and no questions, sometimes called *fixed alternative questions*, to see what the audience believed about the appropriateness of certain procedures used for execution.

> *Fixed alternative questions*: Questions such as true/false or agree/disagree for which there are only two possible responses.

Brett's survey included:

    1. I believe that hanging is cruel and unusual punishment. ___ yes ___no

2. The most humane form of capital punishment is lethal injection. ___ yes ___ no
3. Firing squads should be outlawed in a civilized society. ___ yes ___ no

Brett also used a series of *scale questions* in order to determine the strength of the respondents' attitudes. Questions from his survey included:

1. How strongly do you agree with the statement, "Capital punishment is appropriate in murder cases?"
   ___ Strongly agree
   ___ Mildly agree
   ___ Not sure
   ___ Mildly disagree
   ___ Strongly disagree
2. Do you agree or disagree with using capital punishment for convicted murderers under the age of eighteen?
   ___ Strongly agree
   ___ Somewhat agree
   ___ Undecided
   ___ Somewhat disagree
   ___ Strongly disagree

Scale questions: Questions designed to determine the strength of a respondent's attitude.

In larger audiences where the members are not frequently in the same location, the questionnaire may be a less practical means of accomplishing audience analysis. In these situations sample interviews or focus groups representing the audience may accomplish the same purpose.

In still other situations, the speaker will not know or have a convenient way to contact anyone from the audience except the contact person who arranges the speech. In these cases the speaker will need to ask sufficient audience analysis type questions of this one person to gain an overview of the audience.

At the very least the speaker can accomplish a small degree of audience analysis through the process of *intellectual audience analysis*. Here the speaker mentally infers from what is known about the audience some of the things that are not known. Extreme care must be taken in performing an intellectual audience analysis in order to ensure that the speaker does not stereotype. *Stereotyping* occurs when a characteristic is applied to an entire people group. For instance, declaring, "The audience will not like country music because they are all under thirty." In truth many both under and over thirty appreciate a wide variety of music.

> *Intellectual audience analysis*: Mentally inferring what is known about an audience.

Larry, however, did an effective intellectual audience analysis. He knew from observation that his class was made up primarily of people in the eighteen to twenty-five age bracket, who were 92 percent Caucasian. He further knew that they all were American citizens and had earned high school diplomas. By means of the process of intellectual audience analysis he surmised some important facts about his audience for his speech on "The Civil Rights Movement in America." Larry determined that:

1. None of his audience had experienced the 1960s era movement firsthand.
2. Few in his audience had experienced racial discrimination.
3. Most in his audience knew something about Dr. Martin Luther King Jr.

Because intellectual audience analysis is a very simple process, there is danger that a speaker may ignore the opportunities it affords. To do so is ultimately to yield to the egocentric notion that everyone will see the issues raised in the speech just like the speaker. That assumption is false in nearly every public speaking situation.

Matching the Topic to the Occasion

In addition to matching the topic to the speaker and to the audience, the effective public speaker takes great care to match the topic to the occasion. Two aspects of speaking occasions are particularly important. These are the objective of the speech and the length of time set aside for the speech.

The audience or its representative usually determines the type of public speaking event in advance. That type must be discovered and carefully considered as the speaker matches the topic to the occasion.

Karla gave a very effective speech on "Donating Blood." She explained the need for blood donors and offered impressive statistics on the overwhelming number of college students in America who had never given blood. She ended the speech with an appeal to her classmates to participate in next week's campus blood drive. Karla was surprised when her instructor gave her very low marks on the speech. The assignment had been to deliver a speech to inform, not a speech to persuade. Karla might have focused on the process of drawing the blood or the process that is used for recruiting blood donors if she had carefully considered her topic in light of the objective of the speech for this occasion.

At a March 2003 concert of the country music group Dixie Chicks, the audience expected that the purpose of the event was their entertainment. When lead singer, Natalie Maines, took the opportunity to engage in a political attack on the president of the United States, there were serious repercussions. Fans let it be known that they believed, especially in the days leading up to war in Iraq, that her public speech should have matched the occasion. Later radio stations across America agreed with the audience and joined in the fray by refusing to play the groups' recordings.[5] Matching the speech to the occasion could have avoided these reactions.

In addition to matching the topic to the occasion, the effective speaker must match the topic to the time frame. *Chronemics* is the study of time and expectations concerning time. The time of day when a speech will be delivered is one consideration. A speech at eight o'clock in the morning may require a livelier introduction than one for the same speech delivered later in the day. One speaker even used an introduction with a wake-up activity for an early morning speech.

> *Chronemics*: Study of time and expectations concerning time.

Chronemics also considers the length of the presentation. In the culture of the United States, time is considered a commodity that can be bought and sold, saved or squandered, wasted or used effectively. Time constraints are thus a very important aspect of the public speaking process.

Mike was invited to give a five-minute presentation to the Rotary Club in his hometown as part of the organization's support for local college students. When Mike spoke for twenty-two minutes he severely disrupted the business schedules of several in his audience. As a result, those audience members did not see Mike's speech nearly as positively as they otherwise might have. Mike's argument that he needed more than five

---

5. Mansfield, "The Chicks Ruffle Some Feathers."

minutes to accomplish his task is revealing. That argument says that Mike had failed to match the topic to the occasion with regard to time.

Characteristics of a Thesis Statement

A *thesis statement* is a one sentence summary of what the speaker hopes to accomplish in the speech. It is the big idea of the topic boiled down to a single sentence.[6] Thesis statements have been identified by various descriptive terms such as *central idea*,[7] *specific purpose*,[8] and *specific speech goal*.[9] In every case, however, the guidelines for developing such a statement remain the same. Five characteristics mark the effective thesis statement.

Characteristic #1 Complete Sentence

An effective thesis statement is made up of one complete sentence. Sentence fragments may lead to the speaker lacking the necessary specificity to make the speech clear. Similarly, multiple sentences usually indicate that a narrowing of the topic is still in order.

Jody violated this characteristic when she began to research her speech with the thesis statement "taking a cruise." She began to get bogged down in her research with information about what to take along on a cruise, and even data on the dimensions of some of the best cruise ships. Later Jody rewrote the thesis statement to read, "This speech will inform the audience of three essential steps to selecting a Caribbean cruise." Now she knew precisely what data applied to her speech and what did not.

Characteristic #2 Speech Type

A thesis statement indicates the type of speech. The statement may use synonyms rather that the exact words, but it will reveal whether the speech is designed to inform, persuade, edify, or celebrate.

Harvey began with the thesis statement, "This speech will be about prayer using the ACTS acronym of adoration, confession, thanksgiving and supplication." Harvey failed, in this early attempt, to indicate the type of speech. It cost him time and confusion in the speech development process because he had not been clear about whether his purpose was to inform, persuade, edify, or celebrate. Later, Harvey rewrote the thesis

---

6. Frank, "I'll Show You My Underwear," 14–18.
7. Jaffe, *Public Speaking*, 97–100.
8. DeVito, *The Elements of Public Speaking*, 115–16.
9. Verderber and Verderber, *The Challenge of Effective Speaking*, 58–59.

statement and made it more effective. His final draft read, "This speech will encourage the audience in their prayer life by means of the ACTS acronym of adoration, confession, thanksgiving and supplication." Harvey was clearly working on a speech to edify.

Characteristic #3 Audience Oriented

A thesis statement considers the audience. An effective statement is stated in such a way that what the speaker hopes to accomplish on behalf of the audience is clear. The statement is audience-oriented rather than speaker-oriented.

Gregg began writing a eulogy for his grandfather's funeral with the thesis statement "I will celebrate Grandpa's life by describing three life-changing moments we shared together." Gregg recognized after a few hours of struggle that the speech was more about helping himself through the grief process than offering assistance to his cousins and others in attendance. He revised the statement to conform to characteristic #3. His thesis statement became "This speech of celebration will help the audience deal with Grandpa's death by describing three life-changing moments he and I shared together." Gregg found the difficult public speaking assignment easier because he now had a purpose that involved the audience, and thus was bigger than just himself.

Characteristic #4 Precise Language

A thesis statement uses precise language. Vague terms and figurative expressions are best avoided in order to make the statement effective.

Fran wanted to persuade her classmates that procrastination by college students led to academic difficulties. She developed the thesis "This speech will persuade the audience that when it comes to test preparation, a stitch in time saves nine." She experienced a great deal of difficulty, however, in putting her information into a suitable organizational structure. Part of the problem grew out of the use of metaphoric language in the original statement. Those problems disappeared when she adjusted the statement to, "This speech to persuade will suggest three ways that the audience can avoid the pitfall of procrastination in academic life."

Characteristic #5 Specific Points

Finally, a thesis statement reveals the specifics of the speech. The statement should, when possible, list the main points of the speech. Where that is not possible because of the single sentence limitation, at least the number of main points should be stated.

Les tried to develop a speech to inform with the thesis "This speech will inform the audience about the tons of purchases that can be made on the Internet." Since purchases are not made in tons, this thesis statement uses figurative language. But, in addition, Les had failed to incorporate characteristic # 5—specific points. He found the speech building process went more smoothly when he adjusted his thesis to "This speech will inform the audience about three of the most unusual purchases made recently through eBay."

Correct thesis statement development, which incorporates these five characteristics, is a time consuming and demanding task.[10] Later in the speech building process, however, the time invested pays huge dividends. A comedian quipped, "If you don't know where you're going, you'll get there every time." Nowhere is that statement more true than in the process of researching and organizing a speech. Thus, only when armed with a well-written thesis statement does the effective public speaker turn to the important research task.

The Chapter in Brief

When a speaker faces the opportunity to speak it becomes necessary first to define the type of speech required. Once the speaker has decided whether the speech will inform, persuade, edify or celebrate it is time to select an appropriate topic. Possible sources for generating these preliminary topics include:

- Brainstorming
- Preliminary research
- Current events
- Pre-selected topics
- Audience needs
- Speaker interests

Preliminary topics must then be refined by matching the topic to the speaker, to the audience, and to the specific speaking occasion.

The development of a thesis statement, a specific statement of what the speaker hopes to accomplish in the speech, is the final aspect of deciding on a speech topic. Five characteristics mark the most effective thesis statements. These five are:

10. Darrow, "Using The Big 6," 36.

- The thesis statement is one complete sentence.
- The speech type is indicated in the thesis statement.
- The thesis statement is oriented to the audience not to the speaker.
- Precise language is used to write the thesis statement.
- The points of the speech are listed as precisely as possible in the thesis statement.

Key Terms

- brainstorming
- reframing the alternatives
- audience analysis
- demographic audience analysis
- psychological audience analysis
- situational audience analysis
- intellectual audience analysis
- chronemics
- speech type
- speech topic
- thesis statement
- fixed alternative questions
- scale questions
- stereotyping

For Review and Discussion

1. The student union roundtable group had begun a brainstorming session for a speech on, "I believe the greatest American is ____." With your class or discussion group engage in that same brainstorming exercise. Then prepare a two to three minute speech for delivery to the class on one of the names that emerge from the experience.

2. Jacob described his speech instructor's emphasis on a thesis statement as, "a lot of overblown busy work." Do you agree or disagree? What are some possible pitfalls of not writing an effective thesis statement? What are some advantages to having such a statement?

3. Analyze the thesis statements below with your discussion group or class using the characteristics for a good thesis statement presented in this chapter. Improve those statements that do not follow the

guidelines. Assume the speeches associated with these statements are to be delivered in class in five to seven minutes.

a) This speech will encourage the audience to tithe by presenting three biblical reasons.
b) This speech will teach the audience about life in Cuba.
c) This speech will answer for the audience the question, "Is money or the love of money the root of all evil?"
d) In this speech I want to thank the audience for electing me most likely to succeed.
e) This speech will teach the audience to play the guitar.
f) This speech will remind the audience of my grandmother's exemplary life.
g) Persuade the audience to file their taxes on-line.

Proclamation Practice

Prepare and deliver a two to three minute speech describing one of the following terms:
- brainstorming
- thesis statement
- audience analysis

6

Developing the Speech

Chapter Challenges

A careful reading of Chapter 6 will provide insight into these chapter challenges:

1. What are four commonly used patterns of reasoning?
2. What are some of the common fallacies of reasoning?
3. Compare and contrast the five most common types of supporting materials.
4. Describe the four primary sources of supporting materials.

At the Student Union Roundtable

"How is everyone progressing on the greatest American speech?" asked Belsa of the public speaking study group.

"Now that we have a topic narrowed down and a thesis statement written, the assignment is going much better for me," responded Janelle. She opened her public speaking notebook to show the group her accomplishments.

"I agree," said Cynthia. "I'm finding plenty of information on Dr. Martin Luther King Jr." She sipped her coffee as she looked over Janelle's notes appreciatively.

"Plenty of data on Benjamin Franklin too," agreed Ryan. "I have my speech about ready to start practicing the delivery."

"I practiced last night into a tape recorder," Jess said. "Until then, I was as happy about the abundance of information as all of you seem to be. Not any more."

"What's wrong?" asked Cynthia, noticing the look of anguish on Jess's face.

"My three to five minute speech ran nine minutes and thirty-seven seconds," lamented Jess. "I guess I found too much good information."

"Some serious cutting is in order," advised Belsa. He tried to imitate the stern voice of Dr. Connelly their speech instructor.

"You're right, of course," Jess agreed, grinning at Belsa's imitation. Then getting more serious he continued, "The problem is how to slice that much, and still support my claim that John Kennedy was the greatest American. It's taking me most of the allotted time just to introduce his background and significant accomplishments."

Patterns of Reasoning

Jess's struggle is not uncommon among those who regularly prepare and deliver speeches. He knows what he wants to accomplish in the speech and has recorded that purpose in an effective thesis statement. Developing the speech, however, requires more than that. Jess will need to offer compelling evidence of the appropriateness of his selection of John Kennedy as the greatest American. He will do this by means of an argument. In public speaking an argument is not a heated debate but evidence that demonstrates the thesis statement. The arrangement of the evidence will follow Jess's selected line of reasoning. Usually one of four lines or patterns of reasoning is chosen.

Inductive

Inductive reasoning combines and examines a series of observations in order to arrive at a general conclusion. The pattern requires collecting enough observations as evidence in order to adequately support the general conclusion.

In her speech to persuade, Andrea recommended boycotting a particular retail chain. First, she cited specific evidences leading to that recommendation:

- Evidence #1 The store uses strongly suggestive sexual appeal in its advertising.
- Evidence #2 The store discriminates against minorities.
- Evidence #3 The store offers merchandise at greatly inflated prices.

Andrea then drew a general conclusion; "Therefore, this store practices a worldview that Christians should not support." Andrea used an inductive pattern of reasoning to present her argument.

Sean used the inductive pattern in a speech of introduction. His evidence included:

- Our speaker has traveled around the world.
- Our speaker is in demand on the lecture circuit.
- Our speaker has written several books on tonight's subject.
- Our speaker is considered an expert on the topic.

Sean concluded, "Therefore it is wise to listen carefully to tonight's lecture."

Deductive

In *deductive reasoning* the speaker uses a generally accepted claim in order to reason the truth about a specific claim or claims. For example:

- All Christians attend church.
- Jody is a Christian.
- Therefore, Jody attends church.

The generally accepted claim is sometimes called the *major premise*. The specific example is known as a *minor premise*, while the third statement is called the *conclusion*.

> *Major premise*: Generally accepted claim that is used to begin the process of deductive reasoning.
>
> *Minor premise*: A specific point or example that fits within the major premise in the process of deductive reasoning.
>
> *Conclusion*: The necessary consequence of the major and minor premise in deductive reasoning.

Irene used deductive reasoning in her class devotion designed to encourage chapel attendance among her classmates. Her deductive logic flowed this way:

- Major premise: Worship services benefit Christians.
- Minor premise: Chapel is a worship service.
- Conclusion: Christians would benefit from chapel.

Similarly, when Les delivered a speech to inform on the right to free speech, he used this pattern of deductive reasoning:

- Major premise: All United States citizens are guaranteed freedom of speech.
- Minor premise: The people in this room are United States citizens.
- Conclusion: You are guaranteed free speech.

The speaker who chooses deductive reasoning must establish that there is general agreement on the major premise. When Liz declared eating meat to be harmful in her speech garnering support for animal rights legislation, she failed the general agreement test. Many in her audience simply did not accept the major premise that "red meat kills." Liz would probably have been more successful had she reinforced her major premise before using deductive reasoning.

Causal

Causal reasoning is a pattern that supports a speaker's claim by establishing a cause and effect relationship. It is sometimes referred to as "if/then" reasoning because it assumes that if one factor is present, then another will likely follow.

Marc attempted to persuade his classmates that procrastination had devastating consequences for college students. He used causal reasoning to declare that last minute preparation (cause) led to poor grades (effect).

Michael used a causal pattern in his class devotion. He maintained that a healthy devotional life (cause) leads to more high-quality Christian decisions (effect).

Speakers who use the causal pattern must take great care to avoid a problem known as *false cause*. False cause is an error in reasoning that leads a speaker to conclude that one event caused another when, in fact, there is no causal link.

In his speech to persuade, Les attempted to get his classmates to protest against a tuition hike announced at his school. He declared a causal link between the increase in tuition and the building of a new administration center on the campus. Later, Les discovered that no student tuition and fees had gone into the center. Instead an alum had left instructions in his will, along with enough money, for the new administration center to be built. Les had clearly used a false cause.

Analogical

Analogical reasoning compares two things that have some similar characteristics, and concludes that what is true for one will also be true for the other. It is based on the assumption that when there is some resemblance between two items, the resemblances will be automatically universal.

Candy used analogical reasoning when she attempted to persuade her classmates to sign a petition for à la carte service in the college cafeteria. She declared, "Forcing students to buy a twenty-one meal plan is like the bookstore requiring you to buy the books for every class without recognizing the possibility of sharing a book or buying from an off-campus supplier." Candy correctly noted the similarities between the bookstore and the cafeteria and used analogical reasoning to expand the comparisons and make her point.

Phil attempted to use analogical reasoning to compare two novels by one of his favorite fiction authors, John Grisham. He reasoned, "Every since I read *The Runaway Jury*, I have been anxious to read another of Grisham's accounts of jury manipulation, *The Last Juror*." Phil made the mistake of assuming that the two Grisham books about courtroom juries are both also about jury manipulation. In this case his analogical reasoning is flawed, since the latter Grisham novel has an entirely different theme.

Choosing to reason inductively, deductively, causally, or analogically establishes a preliminary decision in the development of the speech. But regardless of the pattern of reasoning, the speaker will need to exercise great care to avoid the several fallacies of reasoning that tend to plague speakers as they think through data and draw conclusions.

Fallacies of Reasoning

A *fallacy* is a flaw in reasoning that generates the wrong conclusion. It has been estimated that as many as one hundred twenty-five different kinds of fallacies exist.[1] Fallacies should be avoided by public speakers in order to maintain credibility before an audience and remain above reproach ethically. In addition, listeners, as consumers of public address, should learn to identify fallacies and thereby become better prepared to evaluate the validity of a speaker's argument. Six fallacies are the most common.

Name-Calling

Sometimes called the *ad hominem fallacy*, *name-calling* attacks the person holding a position rather than the position itself. In a speech against capital punishment, Bruce referred to those who favored the death penalty as "barbaric murderers." He hoped to convince the audience to agree with his position on capital punishment by undermining those who disagree with him. But such name-calling has no place in ethical public address. It negatively impacts a speaker's credibility and is generally less than convincing.

The ad hominem fallacy moves the audience's thinking out of the arena of ideas. That happened in Bruce's audience as members began to defend themselves and others mentally and, in the process, ignored Bruce's otherwise well thought out points.

Circular Reasoning

A second fallacy, *circular reasoning* assumes as a premise what the speaker actually intends to prove as a conclusion. In his speech to persuade against high-speed driving, Jacob offered an illustration of someone who had driven through campus at a very high rate of speed. He then declared, "No sane person would ever drive at those speeds; that driver was obviously insane."

Samantha offered her own version of circular reasoning when she stated, "Only pagans skip chapel; that is because real Christians want to be in chapel." Samantha had declared the conclusion to be the premise.

---

1. Lucas, *The Art of Public Speaking*, 452.

Slippery Slope

The *slippery slope fallacy* makes the assumption that going the first step in a certain direction will inevitably lead to ultimate disaster in that direction. Calvin declared in his speech to persuade, "The murder of Terri Schiavo is just the first step. Ultimately, anyone who has the flu will be murdered to save the cost of medicine." While many people saw the Schiavo case as a dangerous precedent, most would not hold to the ultimate disaster predicted by Calvin.

In a speech to persuade about the special favors granted to college athletes, Nedra argued, "The idea of a team meal that is so much better than the food offered to others in the cafeteria is repugnant. Eventually, it will lead to all the athletes on this campus being housed downtown at the Carlton, instead of here in the dorms with the rest of us peons." That statement envisions a slippery slope that Nedra would have a hard time supporting with a more rational argument.

"After" Equated with "Causal"

One of the most common fallacies in our culture today is the *after-equated-with-causal fallacy*. This fallacy assumes that just because something occurs chronologically after an event that event is the precipitating cause. Rhonda aced two tests for which she felt less than adequately prepared on the day she wore the red sweater that her favorite aunt had given her. Rhonda declared, "It is my lucky sweater." She associated the passing of tests with the wearing of the sweater. But the fact that the tests came after the sweater wearing had nothing to do with her scores on the tests.

A nationwide example of the after-equated-with-causal fallacy occurred in Italy in the days following the death of Pope John Paul II. Lottery officials there reported a surge in bets using the numbers 2, 21, 37, and 84, after it was reported that the popular pontiff had died on April 2 at 2137 (i.e. 9:37p.m.) local time at the age of eighty-four. Gamblers believed that the numbers some how had been given mystical powers.[2]

Red Herring

The *red herring fallacy*, sometimes called the "smokescreen fallacy," derives its name from the days of fox hunting in England. Before the hunt a smoked herring, which is usually red in color, was dragged around the fields in the area of the hunt. Thus the crops were protected when the dogs

---

2. World, "What are the Odds?" 11.

were thrown off the track of the fox by the extraneous odor. Today the red herring fallacy refers to the introduction of irrelevant arguments, which divert the attention of the audience away from the topic at hand.

In his speech to persuade, Doug asked, "How can we even contemplate spending more money on highway construction when there are thousands of starving children in Africa?" Since there is no real connection between the proposed highway construction and the starvation problem, Doug has introduced a red herring.

Tiffany used a red herring in her campaign for student senate at her university. She said in a campaign speech, "The under-representation of women at all levels of our nation's government must be addressed. A vote for me begins to correct that wrong." In fact, whatever the representation of women in national government, it has nothing to do with Tiffany's university's senate. Further, from a seat on the university senate, Tiffany will not have a forum from which to correct any perceived national social ills.

Either / Or

The *either/or fallacy* frames the alternatives available to a listener in such a way that it appears there are really only two options. The fallacy, when used consciously, assumes that the listener will not recognize and respond to other alternatives.

"Either begin now to play golf on a regular basis, or when you are old and gray you will not have a hobby," Peter said in his speech to persuade. In fact, there are several alternative activities that seniors enjoy.

Advertisers often use the either/or fallacy to promote their products. Implicit in most commercials is the idea that the purchase of the product in question guarantees success, wealth, sex appeal, or a host of other characteristics that may or may not actually be associated with the use of that product. Buyers may either buy the product or forfeit the positive outcomes.

The effective speaker will carefully plan and implement a reasoning style and will avoid the fallacies of faulty reasoning. It will still be necessary, however, to support the arguments of the speech with evidence. Several different evidentiary options exist.

Types of Supporting Materials

Supporting materials are the evidence that the speaker includes in the speech in order to clarify and justify each point. There are several common types of supporting material.

Definitions

A *definition* is a statement providing the exact meaning of a word or phrase. Offering a definition as part of a speech is designed to eliminate ambiguity and confusion in the minds of audience members. It is wise for a speaker never to assume that he or she shares with audience members the same definition of an important term.

In fact, every word and all terms and phrases have at least two meanings. *Denotative meanings* are those that are found in a dictionary. They are the objective definitions that most people agree on. But words also have a *connotative meaning*. That is the personal and subjective meaning of a word. The connotative meaning of a word grows out of an individual's personal experiences. There is never a guarantee of overlap between two people on the connotative meaning of a word.

> *Connotative meaning*: Meanings of words or phrases that grow out of a individual's personal experience.
>
> *Denotative meaning*: Meaning of a word or phrase that is found in a dictionary.

In a class devotion entitled "God as Father," Mia did an excellent job of encouraging the audience to look to God as provider and sustainer. Chelsea who was in Mia's audience did not benefit from the speech in the same way many of her classmates did. That was because Chelsea had grown up in a home with an abusive, alcoholic father. Chelsea's connotative meaning of the word *father* prevented her from fully appreciating Mia's speech.

In reality providing a denotative meaning can never guarantee that an audience's emotional background will not interfere with effective communication. Nevertheless the careful speaker will want to offer denotative definitions from credible sources in an attempt to minimize confusion, clarify meaning, and maximize communication effectiveness.

Statistics

Statistics, a second type of supporting material used frequently in public speaking, are numerical reports of research findings. Numbers make it possible to summarize data and help audiences absorb facts. Statistics serve to synthesize large amounts of information into a more presentable form. In addition, statistics sometimes indicate the enormity of a situation.

For example, in a speech about congestion at the local airport, Renee chose to use statistics instead of telling her own personal story of waiting in line to fly home for spring break. The statistics generalized the problem and made it clear that Renee was not the only one to suffer because of the overcrowding.

One commonly used statistic, the *mean*, allows the speaker to tell the audience the average of a group of numbers. It is calculated by adding together the numbers in a field of data and then dividing by the total number of entries in that field.

> *Mean*: Commonly used statistic that is calculated by adding together the values in a field of data and dividing by the total number of entries in that field.

For example, Tim surveyed his suite mates about the amount of money they spent on last Friday night's date for a light-hearted speech entitled "The Inequity of Chauvinism." He collected the following data: $37.98, $42.75, $26.50, $17.67, $51.50.

Tim calculated the mean amount of money by first adding the five dollar-amounts together. That sum, $176.40, he divided by five, the number of entries in his data field. He arrived at an average of $35.28 spent per man.

The *median* is the middle number in a list that has been placed in rank order. It demonstrates the point at which half of the data is larger and half is smaller. Thus the median score in Tim's study is $37.98, since there are two figures higher and two lower than that amount.

> *Median*: Statistic representing the middle number in a list previously placed in rank order.

A third commonly used statistic is the *mode*. It is the number that occurs most frequently in a set of numbers. It illustrates the most frequent or typical occurrence. Samantha analyzed the scores on the latest public speaking quiz by polling the members of her study group. The seven students reported having earned 98%, 92%, 90%, 90%, 88%, 81%, and 78%. The mode of the scores is 90% since it occurs most frequently in the listing.

Developing the Speech

> *Mode*: Number that occurs most frequently in a set of numbers.

Whatever statistics are used, the speaker must take great care to guarantee the accuracy of the data. A wise man once said, "Figures never lie, but sometimes liars figure." By contrast, Christian public speakers recognize their ethical responsibility to present numerical data truthfully.

In one public speaking class, the assignment was to take a position on the issue of gun control and deliver a speech to persuade articulating that position. Carey delivered a pro-Second Amendment speech, while James argued for banning all handguns in the United States. Both speakers used statistics in support of their position. Carey's data demonstrated that right-to-carry laws reduce crime. James speech used statistics to show that more handguns lead to more crime. Since both "facts" cannot be true, either Carey or James had found and presented inaccurate statistical data. One or the other of the classmates should have researched more carefully, considered their sources more completely, and thus avoided an embarrassing compromise of credibility. Someone simply needed to be more careful about accuracy.

It is also wise to use statistics in moderation. Audiences find it difficult to comprehend numerical support. In addition, they tend to remember it for a shorter period of time than other forms of supporting material.

In a devotional speech entitled "Blessed are the Peacemakers," Andrea listed the United States casualty count for every war from World War I through the War on Terror. Andrea's audience struggled to keep the numbers straight while simultaneously recalling the point Andrea was trying to make. Andrea would have made the same point and better held her audience's attention had she simply summarized the casualties for that entire time period as in excess of two million.

Examples

As Derek delivered his speech to inform on the "Types of Life Insurance," he noticed his audience paying less and less attention. Some looked out the window, while others had an empty glaze in their eyes. That scenario changed abruptly and dramatically, however, when Derek said, "Let me tell you the story of a friend of mine who was able to walk through this insurance maze just in the nick of time." Immediately audience members became more attentive and alert. Derek had witnessed the unmistakable power of *examples* in public address. Examples are specific incidents used to illustrate abstract concepts or ideas.

As Derek discovered, examples capture or recapture the attention of an audience. *Real examples* are the most effective in serving this purpose. Real examples are specific incidents that actually happened. Real examples often enhance the speaker's credibility because the precise time, date, names, and locations of the event can be offered.

> *Real examples*: Actual, real-life incidents that support a point in a speech.

When real examples do not exist in the speaker's past experience or cannot be gleaned from research, *hypothetical examples* are sometimes used. Hypothetical examples describe incidents that did not actually occur in real life but are typical of real life. Sometimes more than one real life example is blended in order to create a hypothetical example.

> *Hypothetical example*: Describes an incident that did not actually occur in real life, but is typical of real life.

When Catherine prepared a persuasive speech on teen pregnancy, she did not feel comfortable revealing the actual identity and circumstances of two high school classmates who became young mothers. Instead she blended the two cases into one hypothetical example. For the sake of integrity she provided verbal clues that the example was hypothetical by saying, "Imagine a teenage girl living in any small town in America."

Narrative

A *narrative* is a story that retells events. Narratives usually convey a symbolic point in addition to simple storytelling. In fact, sometimes the audience recalls the story but misses the point of the story. That only serves to reaffirm the tremendous power of storytelling.[3]

Some speakers are gifted storytellers. They tend to feed off the audience's involvement in the story and embellish the narrative. This sometimes occurs at the expense of good time control. That explains why the

---

3. McDill, The Moment of Truth, 222.

best storytellers find it especially necessary to practice the speech including the narrative account in order to stay within prescribed time limits.

On the other hand, the judicious use of narrative almost always serves to enhance a speech. Just as children perk up at the words "once upon a time," audiences of all ages listen more carefully to a well-told story. Each fall the small town of Jonesborough, Tennessee is flooded with visitors for the National Storytelling Festival. Their presence provides strong testimony to the universal appeal of a well-told story.[4]

Testimony

A fifth type of supporting material is called *testimony*. Testimony, a statement or declaration designed to support or prove something, may originate with a professional or a peer.

In either form testimony is one of the most powerful of all the types of supporting data. That helps to explain why testimony is used in a court of law and also in the church. The power of testimony lies in the fact that the testimony delivers irrefutable evidence.

Professional testimony, also called expert testimony, uses the word of a person considered an authority in a particular field. When Janelle delivered a devotional speech on the major Jewish feasts, she quoted a rabbi whom she had interviewed. The rabbi's words became Janelle's professional testimony. Not only did that testimony support the points of Janelle's speech, but the fact that she had gleaned information by conducting the interview gave Janelle overall credibility on her subject.

> *Professional testimony*: Statement by a professional designed to support or prove a point. Also referred to as "expert testimony."

Ben used *peer testimony* in his speech to persuade urging hunters to complete a hunter safety course. Ben quoted a friend who had been injured in a very serious hunting accident. While the friend was not technically an expert, his personal experience did lend credibility to Ben and his point.

> *Peer testimony*: Statements by someone, other than a professional, designed to support or prove a point.

---

4. Wilson, "11 Great Places to Hear."

Both professional and peer testimony are usually presented in the form of a quotation. The speaker must take great care to determine the accuracy of the quote and to offer appropriate verbal references of the source.

Visual Aids

A sixth type of supporting material, *visual aids*, comprises one of the most powerful tools available to the public speaker. That power stems from visual aid's ability to carry the message of the speaker into the brains of the audience by means of the eyes as well as the ears.

Legal analysts argue that the 1995 acquittal of O. J. Simpson on murder charges stemmed as much from a visual aid as from the compelling arguments of attorney Johnny Cochran. When prosecutor Chris Darden, had Simpson try on the glove purportedly used by the murderer of Simpson's estranged wife, the glove appeared not to fit. The too-tight glove left a persuasive and memorable image in the minds of jurors.[5]

In addition to their persuasive value, visual aids capture and maintain the audience's attention and retention. George W. Bush's State of the Union Address, delivered in January of 2005, was filled with powerful verbal images. One of the most memorable moments, however, was visual and originated, not at the rostrum, but in the balcony. There, an Iraqi woman, Safia Taleb-al-Suhail, whose father was murdered by Sadaam Hussein, offered a hug of comfort and appreciation to Janet Norwood, whose son died in the liberation effort.[6] The audience remembered the strong visual support of the president's speech long after the words had faded away.

But perhaps the most important reason to use visual aids lies not in either their persuasive power or their power to enhance audience attention and retention. Visual aids simply help explain and clarify information. They support a speaker's points and make the complex simple.

Visual aids sometimes take the unusual form of a glove or a hug, or more common forms such as charts, graphs, posters, transparencies, handouts, photographs, objects, models, drawings, maps, video or audio clips, or demonstrations. Regardless of the type of visual aid used, the speaker will benefit from following a few simple rules for visual aid development and delivery.

---

5. Chua-Evans and Gleick, "Making the Case," 48–61.
6. Jones, "Red Ink, Purple Ink," 20–21.

First, visual aids should be large enough to be seen by the entire audience at once. Camille gave her speech to inform on her summer internship in Ukraine. She wanted to focus on the Ukrainian people, and offered as a visual aid a photograph of the family she had stayed with while overseas. The picture, however, was only three inches by five inches. The audience members at the back of the room could not see Camille's visual aid. The impact was lost.

Sometimes beginning speakers attempt to compensate for a small visual aid by passing it through the audience. This technique never works well but is especially inappropriate in larger audiences or for shorter speeches. Had Camille chosen to pass around the photo used in her four to six minute speech, she would have necessarily moved on to point two before the last audience member received the visual aid for point one. As a result, some in Camille's audience would have been forced to choose whether to focus on the visual aid and point one, or the words of point two. Good speakers never give an audience that option. Instead, they compel the audience to listen, and reward that listening with strong points, which enter the brain via eyes as well as the ears.

A second rule for visual aids is that the aids should be simple and clear. Visual aids work best when they communicate one, and only one, point. As a general rule, that point should be so striking that if the speaker displayed the aid without speaking, the message would still come through. Visual aids that require detailed explanations do not work for the speaker. Instead they demand that the speaker work on behalf of the visual aid.

Third, visual aids should be designed for maximum audience impact. They should be clean and neat in appearance, and should display sharp and clear colors. For most student speeches it is not necessary to contract with a professional graphic artist to develop the visual aid. It is necessary, however, to use the best technology available and to take care to produce visual aids that are both accurate and appealing. Experienced speakers recognize that audience members will, to a large extent, measure the credibility of the speaker by the visual presentation.

Finally, visual aids should be an integrated part of the speech. When Robert gave his Christian testimony in a speech of self-introduction, he wanted the audience to experience the open-air chapel at the camp where he committed to Christ. He used his notebook computer and the classroom projection equipment to put a picture of the facility before the entire audience at once. But Robert had not practiced with the visual aid prior to the delivery of his speech. In the time it took for him to call up the image and project it, his audience shifted nervously. Robert had allowed his visual aid to be an add-on rather than a vital part of the speech.

When a good speaker practices these four rules for visual aids, the result is a presentation where visual aids become one of the most compelling of all available supporting materials.

Sources of Supporting Materials

Regardless of which types of supporting materials are used, the speaker will need to find these materials. Doing research for a speech involves discovering the supporting material necessary to make the points of that speech. The discovery process generally will lead the speaker to one of five reservoirs of supporting material.

Experiential Sources

Experienced speakers recognize that they already have a vast knowledge base that has grown out of their previous experiences. Once the speaker has selected a topic and written a thesis statement, contemplation begins about existing knowledge of the subject matter. Often the experiences of the speaker provide materials for the speech directly. These are referred to as *experiential sources*.

Lynn decided to do her speech to inform on baking chocolate-chip cookies. She had a recipe for wonderful chocolate-chip cookies that family members had handed down for several generations. Since Lynn had used this recipe numerous times in the past, her own experience became her most bountiful source of information.

On other occasions the experiences of the speaker do not directly apply to the topic at hand, but they do serve to streamline the research process. Barry's speech instructor assigned a speech to inform on the stock market crash of 1929. Obviously, as a twenty-year-old college sophomore he had no direct experience upon which to draw. Barry did recall, however, an elderly gentleman who attended his church and who often told depression-era stories. Barry contacted the man and set up an interview, which yielded a wealth of first-hand information. Barry's experiences led him to a very productive primary source.

Printed Sources

The college or university library usually houses the most comprehensive collection of supporting materials available to the speaker. Most campus libraries offer orientation tours and seminars designed to help students become familiar with the resources and how to access them.

Much of the information available in the library has been converted to electronic storage of late. Still, many researchers recommend doing a final check of important information in print form, since the accuracy of printed data is more easily confirmed. And some sources usually found in the reference section remain only in print or "hard" copy. The *print sources* available to speech researchers in most libraries include those enumerated below.

- *Almanacs* are books of data and facts. *The World Almanac and Book of Facts* is one example. So is *The Time Almanac.* A speaker might use an almanac to discover the population of Juneau, Alaska, or the year in which Andrew Jackson became President.

- *Atlases* are collections of maps. Often these maps are specialized around a particular theme, such as *The Harper Collins Concise Atlas of the Bible* or Rand McNally's *The Road Atlas of the United States, Canada and Mexico.* A speaker may want to use an atlas to discover things like the distance from Philadelphia to Salt Lake City or to compare the size of the oceans.

- *Biographical collections* are compilations of biographical sketches on selected people. An entire series of *Who's Who* books provide one example. One student, tracing her family tree, came across the biographical collection *Oakwood, Ohio Past and Present,* which contained a sketch of her great-grandfather. Speech researchers commonly discover such specialized biographical collections.

- *Commentaries* are books of explanatory notes or insights. Bible commentaries, such as the multi-volume *Beacon Bible Commentary* or the single volume *The New Bible Commentary: Revised,* are among the examples. A speaker will usually consult a commentary after doing inductive Bible study during the preparation phase of a speech to edify.

- *Dictionaries* are books of information about words. *Webster's New Unabridged Universal Dictionary* is a general dictionary of the entire English language. Such general dictionaries offer definitions, spellings, derivations, and pronunciations. One specialized type of dictionary, the Bible dictionary, contains information about the words used in Scripture. *The Interpreter's Dictionary of the Bible* is just one of many high-quality biblical dictionaries.

- *Encyclopedias* are still available in many libraries in print form, although many researchers choose to use them in electronic form today. Encyclopedias offer articles on a great variety of topics. Just the first volume of *World Book Encyclopedia,* for example, covers topics from Aachen (an industrial city in Germany) to the mineral azurite.

- *Indexes* consider hundreds of periodicals and point the speech researcher to the particular issue that has information on the topic under review. The *Reader's Guide to Periodical Literature* indexes magazines. More academic material is indexed in *The Social Sciences Index* or *The Humanities Index.*

- *Journals* are periodicals that cover a specialized subject matter from an academic perspective. For example, *The Quarterly Journal of Speech* covers the latest developments in the study of rhetoric. One often quoted journal, *The Journal of the American Medical Association,* reports on the latest studies and advancements in health and medical science.

- *Magazines* usually offer a more popularized content than journals. Some, such as *Time, Newsweek,* or *World,* cover a wide array of topics. Others are more specialized, such as *Computer World,* or *Sports Illustrated.*

- *Newspapers* both local and national are offered in many libraries. The newspaper provides current information, or when used in conjunction with an index, can help the speaker discover information from a historical perspective.

- *Quotation collections* are compilations of quotations from historical and contemporary figures. Usually, such collections are arranged by topic. One popular example is *Bartlett's Familiar Quotations*, with more than twenty-five thousand quotations. *A Treasury of Jewish Quotations* provides a more specialized example.

- *Yearbooks* summarize the activities of the past year or offer certain kinds of information about the current year. For example, *Statistical Abstract of the United States* is published by the United States Bureau of the Census and provides numerical facts on a wide array of subjects that relate to American life.

Developing the Speech

Electronic Sources

Many of the sources available in a library in print form are also available as *electronic sources*. For example, editions of most newspapers are available online. In addition, LexisNexis provides access to more than thirty-two thousand legal, news, and business sources at one electronic location.

Most colleges and universities have a computerized search system for their holdings. Often the typical library is also associated with several other libraries in a community or, a consortium. All of the holdings of the several institutions may be searched simultaneously.

Databases are collections of information stored electronically. Databases can usually be accessed through the library system as well. Often these databases are specialized by field of study. For example, ERIC (Educational Resources Information Center) focuses on scholarly papers in the humanities. But, some databases are more general. ProQuest Research Library indexes more than two-thousand general and scholarly journals. Either ProQuest or the very similar, Academic Search Premier is a valuable aid to finding scholarly material on thousands of subjects. Full text databases offer the complete article from the journal, magazine, or research report where it first appeared. In other cases databases offer only an *abstract*. An abstract is a brief summary of the complete text.

Databases: Collections of information stored electronically.

Search engines index Web pages from the World Wide Web and scan them for the information that the speech researcher requests. The most commonly used search engine is Google (www.google.com), which provides access to more than three billion current Web sites.[7] Even the best search engines however, explore only a fraction of the information available on the Web.[8]

Speaker Developed Sources

Speaker developed sources encompass the various ways that a speaker generates supporting material. *Interviews* and *questionnaires* are the two primary types of speaker developed sources.

---

7. Levy, "The World According To Google," 46–51.
8. Hock, *The Extreme Searchers Guide*, 21–22.

> *Interview*: A meeting between a speaker and a person from whom that speaker seeks information.
>
> *Questionnaire*: A set of written questions designed to gain data for a speech.

Gina developed a speech to inform on the use of boot camps as an alternative to traditional incarceration for teenage offenders.[9] She wanted to include the point of view of local law enforcement professionals. A detective in the sheriff's department in her county agreed to an interview. Gina prepared for the interview, by developing a list of questions in advance. Then she arrived punctually for the interview, and spent only a few moments visiting cordially with the detective before asking her first question. She was careful to let the detective do most of the talking while she accurately recorded the responses. After asking her questions, she briefly summarized what she had learned and thanked the detective for his time. Later Gina dropped him a brief note to once again express appreciation for the information.

Ruth used a survey to glean supporting information for her persuasive speech encouraging audience members to take part in a short-term mission trip. Since her campus was small she was able to send her questionnaire to every enrolled student via the free campus mail system. She received a 20 percent response. The data indicated how many students had already participated in such a trip, and Ruth's follow-up questions provided information on where participants had traveled, what mission's sending agencies they had affiliated with, and what kinds of work they were able to accomplish.

Both Gina and Ruth used the approach of many public speakers. When the supporting material they needed was unavailable, they simply did whatever was necessary to generate the data.

---

9. Hubbard and Smith, "Offender System Shines."

The Chapter in Brief

Four primary patterns of reasoning, including inductive, deductive, causal, and analogical are available to the public speaker. Regardless of the pattern that is chosen for developing the arguments of the speech, six common fallacies of reasoning must be avoided. These fallacies are

- Name Calling
- Circular Reasoning
- Slippery Slope
- "After" Equated with "Causal"
- Red Herring
- Either/Or

The types of supporting materials appropriate for making the point of a speaker's argument will vary from one speech to another. Supporting material types that are available to the speaker include:

- Definitions
- Statistics
- Examples
- Narrative
- Testimony
- Visual Aids

The problem of researching the speech is always the same. Where can the speaker find the resources needed to make his or her points? Four sources of supporting materials encompass the primary ways by which that question is answered. These sources are

- Experiential Sources
- Printed Sources
- Electronic Sources
- Speaker Developed Sources

Key Terms

Use the list below to test your knowledge of the vocabulary introduced in this chapter.

- argument
- inductive reasoning
- deductive reasoning
- major premise
- minor premise

- causal reasoning
- false cause
- analogical reasoning
- fallacy
- definition
- denotative meaning
- connotative meaning
- statistics
- mean
- median
- mode
- real examples
- hypothetical examples
- narrative
- databases
- almanacs
- atlases
- biographical collections
- dictionaries
- encyclopedias
- indexes
- journals
- quotation collections
- yearbooks
- electronic sources
- print sources
- experiential sources
- speaker developed sources
- abstract
- search engine
- questionnaires
- interviews
- red herring fallacy
- professional testimony
- commentaries
- peer testimony
- slippery slope fallacy
- circular reasoning
- ad-hominem fallacy

For Review and Discussion

1. Which of the four types of reasoning is most common in a political speech? Which is most common in a sermon? Describe examples you have seen of the other types.
2. Do visual aids ever detract from a speech? Under what circumstances are visual aids most effectively used?
3. What are the advantages of using experiential sources? What are some problems you envision with using experiential sources? How are these problems best avoided?

Proclamation Practice

Prepare for delivery in class a three to five minute speech entitled, "Finding Materials in the Campus Library." The speech could be a verbal tour of the facility or an explanation of what resources are available for the development of a speech.

7

Designing the Speech

Chapter Challenges

A careful reading of Chapter 7 will provide insight into these chapter challenges:
1. What are the four main purposes of a speech introduction?
2. Describe seven processes by which an introduction may gain attention.
3. List five pitfalls to avoid in developing a speech introduction.

4. What are transitions? Describe three specialized transitions used by speakers.
5. What are the four main purposes of a speech conclusion?
6. List four pitfalls to avoid in developing a speech conclusion.
7. Identify the difference between an outline and a manuscript and between a preparation outline and a presentation outline.

At the Student Union Roundtable

"T minus twenty-three hours and counting." Ryan grinned as he joined the others already assembled around the student union roundtable. "Tomorrow I deliver my speech to inform in class. Except for a few finishing touches it's ready to go."

"I hope what you're calling finishing touches are about delivery practice," said Cynthia. "Twenty-three hours is not much time for anything more."

"Right," Ryan agreed, "delivery practice, and also to write the introduction and conclusion."

"You don't have an introduction yet?" asked Belsa with surprise.

"Or a conclusion?" chimed in Janelle accusingly.

"Give the guy a break." Jess defended Ryan. "If he has a quality speech all written and ready to go, the introduction and conclusion can almost be done on the way to class."

"I couldn't do it that way and be effective," argued Jannelle. "In preparation for giving my speech last week, I practiced my introduction more than any other part of the speech."

"Introductions, maybe," Jess hedged. "But conclusions are best done impromptu at the end of the speech. That way you can read the audience and clarify points they missed or build on the ones they seemed to get."

The group broke into a lively debate about the importance of introductions and conclusions in speech preparation. There seemed to be little consensus on the matter.

Primacy and Recency

Significant questions have grown out of the round table discussion about the importance of speech introductions and conclusions. In fact, an effective speech body can be rendered useless without a well-written and well-rehearsed introduction and conclusion. Research clearly indicates that the first and last things that a listener hears will carry greater impact and be retained longer than what comes in between.[1]

On the one hand, the theory of the *primacy effect* states that the first thing heard has the longest lasting and greatest impact.[2] By contrast the theory of the *recency effect* declares that the last thing, or most recent heard, stays with the hearer longer and has the strongest impact. Controversy reigns between proponents of the two principles over which is the most powerful, with some research indicating that the way the information is initially received by a listener explains the difference.[3] All agree, however, that the first and last elements to which a listener is exposed have far more impact than anything that lies between.

When applied to public speaking, theories of primacy and recency indicate that the introduction and conclusion represent the most important parts of a speech. As a result, most experienced speakers spend a great deal of time preparing and practicing these vital components of their speech. In addition to lasting impact, introductions and conclusions are important elements of the overall structure of the speech. Speech design, therefore, carefully considers both.

Introductions

The introduction of a speech impacts the audience through primacy. Therefore the effective speaker will want to ensure effective introductions. The first step in accomplishing such introductions includes a careful examination of an introduction's purposes, the processes by which an effective introduction is accomplished, and strict avoidance of several pitfalls that often plague speech introductions.

Introduction Purposes

The introduction of a speech serves four main purposes. These include:

- Gain audience attention
- Compel the audience to listen
- Establish speaker credibility
- Preview the speech

Mike decided to give his speech to inform on the characteristics and differences between the largest of the "great" cats. He had held a lifelong

---

1. Golob and Starr, "Serial Position Effects in Auditory Event," 40–53.
2. Oberauer, "Understanding Serial Position Curves," 469–84.
3. Seiler and Engelkamp, "Role of Item-Specific Information," 954–65.

interest in the animals and had collected a significant amount of information. Mike could have chosen a simple introduction, such as "Today I intend to inform you about the characteristics and differences between the four largest 'great' cats."

Instead Mike worked hard at developing a more effective and compelling introduction. He recognized that his introduction should serve all four of the main purposes of an effective introduction. So Mike carefully wove these four elements into a comprehensive and effective introduction. He began his speech by saying, "Since our university mascot is the wildcat, I've heard most of you cheer for the Wildcats at athletic events. But the term Wildcat does not just refer to a basketball star. In fact, Wildcat is a loosely used term that can be applied to any species of non-domesticated cat. It often is used to refer to the smaller and less distinct North American cats. But it is also appropriate for the much larger "great" cats."

"Since I was a very small boy I have had an affinity for these great cats. Any TV show, book, or Web site about them intrigues me. As a result, I have collected a great deal of information about their characteristics and their differences."

"Today I want to tell you about four big cats starting with the largest cat in the world and moving to the smaller."[4]

With this introduction Mike captured the attention of the audience. He related the speech to university athletics, which was something the audience understood and found interesting. He also compelled the audience to listen. The clear and concise content of the introduction as well as the ease and enthusiasm of delivery caused the audience to focus on what Mike had to say.

In addition, Mike established his own credibility to speak on the subject of larger cats. He spoke of the long period of time he had studied the topic and alluded to the expertise that he had gained over the years.

Finally, Mike previewed the speech. The audience knows to expect a discussion on four of the large cats. They anticipate that the result will be an overview of the animal's characteristics as well as comparisons between the four. As a result of Mike's preview statement the audience even realizes that he will begin with the largest and move to the smallest of the four animals.

Mike accomplished the four important purposes of an introduction and did it with a minimum of words. Experts suggest that the introduc-

---

4. Snedeker, "The Great Cats" (classroom speech, Indiana Wesleyan University, Marion, IN, Spring, 2005).

tion should occupy only 10 to 15 percent of the total speech.[5] That means that in a six-minute speech the speaker must seek to accomplish all four of the vital introduction components in thirty-six to fifty-four seconds. Clearly, the introduction must be well thought out, carefully planned, and diligently rehearsed.

Introduction Processes

Accomplishing so much in so brief a time requires the speaker to select an introduction process that communicates well. Speakers generally select one of seven introductory processes. These seven include:

- Visual Aids
- Humor
- Questions
- Narrative
- Startling Statement or Fact
- Current Event
- Quotations

Visual Aids

Sometimes speakers draw attention to the topic by displaying a visual aid or playing an audio aid. Ming began her speech on origami by displaying several elaborate paper-folding creations she had already finished. Harvey began a speech on his favorite composer by playing a few seconds of a CD. Ike shared a videotape of a hockey game that had erupted into a major fight as a way to introduce his speech on violence in sports.

Humor

The use of humor also may serve to draw the audience's attention to the speech and to the speaker. In addition, humor serves to lighten the situation thus putting both the speaker and the audience members at ease. Humor should always be tasteful and appropriate and should focus on the topic at hand. While random joke telling may capture the attention of the audience initially, that attention is just as quickly lost when the speaker gets down to the more serious business of the topic at hand. An exception may be humor about the speaker, sometimes called "self-deprecating humor." Such humor makes fun of the self and thus serves to build rapport with the audience. It seems to hold audience members' attention even after the joke has passed.

5. Sellnow, *Confident Public Speaking*, 202.

Questions

Questions sometimes serve to gain the audience's attention and arouse their curiosity about the rest of the speech. Either *rhetorical questions* or *participation questions* are the most common types used.

Rhetorical questions are questions designed for audience members to answer mentally, not out loud. Care must be taken to assure that the audience understands that the question is rhetorical. One speaker, who had several small children in her audience, received a verbal answer to her rhetorical question. Fortunately, she recovered quickly and without embarrassing either the young audience member or his parents.

> *Rhetorical question*: Questions designed for audience members to answer mentally.
>
> *Participation questions*: Questions designed for audience members to answer either verbally or nonverbally.

Participation questions, by contrast, are questions designed for audience members to answer either verbally or nonverbally. Sue Ellen used a participation question for her speech on skydiving when she solicited a show of hands, asking, "How many of you have ever been skydiving?" Shawn sought a verbal response to his participation question in a speech about welfare reform. He began his speech with, "What do you think of when I say the word *welfare*?" Shawn waited several seconds until an audience member called out a single-word response. Others quickly followed.

At least one professional speaker suggests singling out an audience member with an attention getting question.[6] While such a device will gain the attention of everyone, care must be taken to avoid embarrassing the target of the question.

Narrative

Narrative or storytelling is a great way to capture and hold an audience's attention. That is because almost everyone loves to hear a good story. Some maintain that narrative is the best way to communicate, especially in speeches to edify.[7] Regardless of the type of speech narratives should relate closely to the topic.

---

6. Wilder, *7 Steps To Fearless Speaking*, 67.
7. Wangerin, "Making Disciples by Sacred Story," 66–69.

Startling Statement or Fact

A startling statement or fact can also serve to gain the attention of the audience. Michelle began her speech describing a recent vacation in France by greeting the audience in French. Juan advocated financing college education by "selling yourself." "I don't mean prostitution," he clarified, "but plasma."

Sometimes the startling statement involves the use of statistics. The effective speaker must always take great care to insure the accuracy of any numbers used in the speech.

As with all of the attention getting devices, it is essential that the startling statement or fact relate directly to the topic at hand. Karen tried to use a startling statement in the form of one word. She stepped to the podium, took a deep breath, and said, "Sex . . . Now that I have your attention let me share with you my speech today on how to avoid the delays often encountered on our campus when pre-registering for next fall's classes." The audience felt tricked by her gimmicky approach. On the other hand, for a speech on the use of sensual appeal in advertising, her one word attention getter may have been very effective.

Current Event

A current event, especially one that has already captivated the attention of the audience outside the speech event, often serves as an effective way to gain attention for the speech. Students often marvel at the brevity of the introduction of Franklin D. Roosevelt's "Day of Infamy" speech. Coming just one day after the Japanese attack on Pearl Harbor, he needed only a few words to focus the thinking of the audience. Similarly, campus events, national elections, natural disasters, or community accomplishments may all be ready-made attention getting devices.

Quotations

Finally, relevant quotations may aid the speaker in gaining audience attention. Quotations may come from famous people or a friend or relative who has a proverbial saying on a particular topic. The careful speaker will not overlook song lyrics, poetry, or television and movie scripts as sources of attention gaining quotes. It is important to make sure that the quote is relevant to the topic and expresses the desired tone for the speech. Also, the source of the quote must be clearly stated and delivered in such a way that the audience recognizes that the quotation is not the speaker's own original words.

Using one of these seven processes for introduction will aid the speaker in accomplishing the introduction purpose. In fact, careful use nearly guarantees a successful introduction provided the pitfalls of introductions are strenuously avoided.

Introduction Pitfalls

Several common practices of beginning speakers become pitfalls when left unchecked. These are the five don'ts of speech introductions.

Don't False Start

"Before I begin, I'd like to say . . . " Such a statement at the beginning of a speech becomes an introduction to the introduction or a false start. Instead of capturing an audience's attention, it signals that it is not yet the time for listening. Effective speakers, by contrast, make the first word out of their mouths clear and compelling as well as on topic.

Don't Apologize

"I really don't feel very well prepared for this speech, but . . . " is an introductory apology. So is "I've been sick and my voice is weak, so please bear with me." These or comparable statements alert the audience to the fact that the speech may be less than enthralling. Good speakers believe that they have something vitally important to say, and they communicate that confidence to their audience.

Don't Read

Effective speakers never read the introduction of a speech. Reading at any point in a speech tends to distract an audience. Reading the introduction may prove disastrous. Instead the best speakers rehearse their introduction over and over again. They usually stop short of complete memorization in order to avoid sounding mechanical and detached. They do, however, know exactly what they intend to say and how they intend to say it.

Don't Switch Topics

The attention getting section of a speech introduction should be closely and carefully related to the topic of the speech. Good speakers never use a device solely to gain attention and then switch to the real topic at hand. Instead they carefully analyze every word of the all-important introduction in order to be sure it relates to the topic and supports the thesis statement of the speech.

Don't Over Dramatize

Sometimes beginning speakers work so hard on gaining the attention of the audience that they loose sight of the importance of gaining rapport with the audience. They may slip into Broadway actor mode and leave the audience wondering what character is being portrayed. Effective speakers, by contrast, recognize the importance of being themselves. They feel passionate about their topic and convey that passion. But they never turn off the audience with phony melodrama.

Transitions

Transitions are words, phrases, or sentences in a speech that act as bridges linking the main parts of the speech. Sometimes transitions are used to link the introduction with the body of the speech. On other occasions they link the main points within the body. Sometimes transitions join sub-points to a main point. Still other transitions link the body to the conclusion of the speech.

Some basic transitions merely follow the outline of the speech. In such cases the words *first*, *second*, *third* are the key words that provide transition. At other times, the transitions provide a more creative way to signal moving from one point to another. For example, in Jonathan's speech to inform entitled "A Tour of the Library," he moved from one main point to another by saying, "Come along with me now as we climb the stairs to the second floor and move among the regular stacks."

Experienced speakers often use three specialized transitions in order to help the listener follow the design of the speech. *Internal previews*, *internal summaries*, and *signposts* each meet specialized transitional needs.

Internal Previews

Internal previews appear in the body of the speech and explain what the speaker intends to convey next. They prove especially useful when approaching a main point that includes several sub-points. When Billy gave a speech to edify on the twenty-sixth chapter of Acts he made an internal preview as a part of the transition to a new point in the body of the speech. "Now that we have noted the background of Paul's statements before Agrippa, let's look at the three main sections of the words Paul spoke." Billy prepared the audience to listen by alerting them to the next point, containing three sub-points, that he planned to develop.

Internal Summaries

Internal summaries are the opposite of internal previews in that they are statements in the body of the speech that summarize a point or points already discussed. Internal summaries are especially helpful where a just completed point contains especially complex or important data.

Internal summaries also may be used to benefit the audience's retention of main points by reinforcing those points through repetition. Molly used an internal summary coupled with an internal preview in her speech comparing Christian higher education with that received at a state supported school. She summarized between the two points, "Thus far we have seen four advantages to attending a Christian college or university. Now let's look at four corresponding disadvantages."

Jeremy used an internal summary in his speech on avoiding procrastination. He said, "So you see, there are three primary reasons students offer for postponing the work on their assignments."

Signposts

A third specialized transition is called the signpost. Signposts are words or statements that point the way to where the speaker is going in a speech. They also serve to remind the audience of where the speaker is in the delivery process. "Let's examine the third of the five steps in the process" is a signpost. It notes that the speaker is moving to the third point and reminds the audience to anticipate a total of five points.

One very common signpost is the phrase "in conclusion." Some public speaking experts suggest this, or a similar signpost, as a means of warning the audience that the speech is ending.[8] One has only to engage in a moment of self-reflection, however, to recognize the negative effect of this particular signpost. Imagine a lecture class where the professor says, "Now let me just summarize what I've said over the last fifty minutes, and we will be done." Students will immediately begin to put away notebooks and gather up personal belongings. These words have acted as a signpost that signals, "Stop listening! The important part is over." Public speakers never want to impart such a signal to their audience. Instead they do whatever is necessary to continue to compel the audience to listen right up through the very last word. Good speakers never encourage the audience to mentally check out early. They want to hold the audience through the conclusion because there are several important functions of a good speech conclusion.

---

8. Lucas, *The Art of Public Speaking*, 242–44.

Conclusions

The conclusion is a vital part of the design of the speech. It is the last thing the audience will hear from the speaker on the subject, and in light of the recency effect, the conclusion may be the most memorable portion of the speech. The speech conclusion should be brief. Usually 5 to 10 percent of the total speech is sufficient for an adequate conclusion.[9] The effective speaker will use this time to accomplish four important purposes while avoiding an equal number of pitfalls.

Conclusion Purposes

The four key functions or purposes of the conclusion of a speech include:

- Reinforce the thesis
- Summarize the points
- Refer to the introduction
- Make the speech memorable

Reinforce the Thesis

Since the conclusion is the last opportunity to drive home the main idea of the speech the speaker will want to once more reinforce the thesis statement. Some beginning speakers avoid this restatement, believing it is too redundant and thus boring to the audience. In reality audiences appreciate the reminder. The concept can be summed up this way:

- In the introduction tell them what you will tell them.
- In the body tell them.
- In the conclusion tell them what you told them.

Summarize the Points

One aspect of telling them what you told them involves summarizing or reiterating the main points of the speech. That does not mean repeating everything that has been previously stated. A simple summary is adequate.

Refer to the Introduction

One of the most important aspects of the conclusion of a speech involves referring back to the introduction. This provides closure in the minds of audience members. Such a referral makes the speech a package or a complete unit. In addition, such a reference rewards the audience for taking the time to listen to the speech. Audience members made a decision to lis-

---

9. Lucas, *The Art of Public Speaking*, 247.

ten to the speech sometime during the introduction. That decision, based upon the attention getting device of the introduction, is reinforced when the introduction is alluded to in the conclusion.

In Mike's speech described earlier, he used such a device when he concluded, "So the next time you go to the gym to cheer for the University Wildcats, remember the four wildcats we've discussed this afternoon."[10]

Make the Speech Memorable

Mike's statement also provided a way for the speech to be reinforced each time an audience member attended a university basketball game. He had found a way to make the speech memorable. The most effective speeches are those that audience members retain for a longer than usual period of time. In fact, audience retention is generally very low over the long haul. One pastor noted, "If anyone mentions specifics of the Sunday morning sermon by Sunday night, I've done well. On those rare occasions when it happens at the mid-week service on Wednesday, I've done a phenomenal job." Sometimes a quotation, example, challenge, or call to specific action makes the speech memorable for a longer period of time.

Conclusion Pitfalls

Conclusions in particular and speeches in general become more memorable when the speaker avoids four common pitfalls. These include:

- Don't apologize
- Don't introduce new information
- Don't just stop
- Don't drone on

Don't Apologize

Lisa ended her speech with the statement, "Well, I guess I've rambled on about this long enough." In reality Lisa had delivered a fairly effective speech up to that point. That effectiveness was seriously minimized, however, by her reference to "rambling on." Good speakers never use the conclusion to apologize for their topic, their thesis, their lack of preparation, or their delivery. They instead do the best job

---

10. See note 4.

possible and assume that the audience has benefited.

Don't Introduce New Information

The conclusion should act as a summary and reinforcement of material already presented. It should not become a forum for new or additional points of the speech

The only exception to this prohibition involves the call to action of a persuasive speech. Tyler provided the phone number for the state representative in his speech designed to persuade the audience to support a particular legislative effort. That number was appropriately a part of his speech conclusion, since it involved a clear and specific call to action.

By contrast, Brian outlined "Five Steps to a Do-It-Yourself Oil Change" in his speech to inform. He saved step number six for the conclusion of his speech, reasoning that it would give the point more emphasis. Brian's new information confused the audience as to whether the process involved five or six steps. He should have avoided introducing new information in the speech conclusion.

Don't Just Stop

Carmen had not had time to prepare a conclusion for the expository lesson that she used for class devotions. She reached the end of her preparation, paused for a moment, shrugged her shoulders, and said, "I guess that's about it." Carmen had to just stop her speech because she had not developed a suitable exit strategy.

In the same public speaking class, Adam experienced the identical problem. Instead of the "guess that's about it" line, he simply sat down. He had finished his third point but had not summarized, reinforced the thesis, or reminded the audience of his introductory attention getter. His speech proved to be memorable, but not for the right reasons.

Don't Drone On

The flip side of the "just stop" coin might be termed "droning on." One church member, commenting on a pastor's Sunday morning message, noted, "That was three of the best sermons I've heard in a long time." Sometimes a well-prepared speech is actually too long for the occasion. At other times, however, the sense of going on and on and on comes because the speaker has not developed an effective conclusion. The best conclusions and the best speeches always leave the audience wanting to hear more.

Outlines

An *outline* is a brief synopsis or skeleton of the speech. It assists the speaker in designing or delivering the speech. An outline should not be confused with a *manuscript*, which is a word for word transcript of the speech. The best speakers always create an outline, but they may or may not write a manuscript of their speech. Two distinct types of outlines exist. These are *preparation outlines* and *presentation outlines*.

> *Manuscript*: Word for word text of a speech.

Preparation Outlines

A preparation outline helps the speaker prepare the speech and check for all of the essential elements. A preparation outline should include the title of the speech and the thesis statement. It clearly shows the introduction, body, transitions, and conclusion. Within the body section of a preparation outline appears each point along with the various sub-points. The entire outline is completed in full sentences.

Presentation Outline

The presentation outline, sometimes called a speaking outline, aids the speaker in delivery of the speech. It rarely uses full sentences but instead highlights a few key words or phrases designed to help the speaker avoid a memory lapse in delivering the speech. Some speakers prefer note cards to paper for the presentation outline. Either way, the outline should be typed or written large enough to be seen at a glance. It should be on only one side of a page to avoid flipping a page and thus diverting the audience's attention. Some speakers actually include gestures or movements that they intend to employ on the presentation outline itself. They thus remind themselves of the key role of delivery in the overall public speaking process. That role is the subject of Chapter 8.

The Chapter in Brief

Research on primacy and recency suggests that the first and the last thing a listener hears have a profound and longer lasting impact. As a result, good public speakers focus a great deal of their preparation energy on the introductions and conclusions of their speeches.

The introduction of a speech serves four primary purposes. These include:

- Gain audience attention
- Compel the audience to listen
- Establish speaker credibility
- Preview the speech

Usually, speakers accomplish these purposes by means of a visual aid, humor, questions, narration, a startling statement or fact, reference to a current event, or a relevant quotation.

The best introductions come from speakers who avoid introduction pitfalls by reminding themselves:

- Don't false start
- Don't apologize
- Don't read
- Don't switch topics
- Don't over dramatize

Transitions are the bridges by which a speaker walks an audience from one main section of the speech to another. Frequently, a speaker will use internal previews, internal summaries, or signposts, which are specialized transitions.

Conclusions serve four primary purposes, including:

- Reinforcing the thesis
- Summarizing the points
- Referring to the introduction
- Making the speech memorable

As with introductions, there are several conclusion pitfalls into which speaker's frequently slip. The most effective speakers remember:

- Don't apologize
- Don't introduce new information
- Don't just stop
- Don't drone on

Finally, a speaker should complete the speech design by means of a preparation outline. Once the preparation has been accomplished, many speakers choose a presentation outline to assist in delivery. Presentation outlines are much briefer than preparation outlines and may vary according to the style and experience of the speaker.

Key Terms

Use the list below to test your knowledge of the vocabulary introduced in this chapter.

- primacy effect
- recency effect
- rhetorical question
- participation question
- signposts
- transitions
- internal previews
- internal summaries
- preparation outline
- presentation outline

For Review and Discussion

1. At the student union roundtable, a debate developed about the importance of introductions and conclusions. What position would you take in that debate? Why?
2. Which of the seven processes used by speakers to build effective introductions do you find most compelling? Which do you believe is least effective?
3. Which of the purposes of a speech conclusion is most important? Defend your answer.

Proclamation Practice

Use your most recent research paper for another course as the body of a speech. Write an introduction and conclusion that will enable you to deliver the paper as a speech. Deliver the speech in class in the time frame assigned by your instructor.

8

Delivering the Speech

Chapter Challenges

A careful reading of Chapter 8 will provide insight into these chapter challenges:

1. Compare and contrast the four principal styles of speech delivery.
2. Describe the five dos of effective speech delivery.
3. Describe the five don'ts of effective speech delivery.

At the Student Union Roundtable

"Where's Cynthia?" asked Janelle as she joined the study group at the student union roundtable. "Everyone else has arrived."

"She missed Biblical Literature this morning," Belsa offered. "Maybe she is sick."

"Not sick," corrected Ryan, "just busy. She is memorizing her speech to inform for class tomorrow. She told me she has poor memorization skills, and trying to memorize a six-minute speech is driving her crazy."

"So why is she memorizing anyway?" asked Jess. "I can't see going to all that work for one speech. I plan to just read mine."

"Boring!" declared Jannelle. "I hate being read to."

"Notes, my friends, that is the answer," Ryan said. "Just take a few notes and wing it."

"I'd wing a certain failing grade," Belsa replied. "Notes just don't provide enough help in the likely event that my mind goes blank and I slip into a catatonic state, forgetting everything."

Janelle shook her head as she looked at the puzzled faces around the table. "It sounds as if we still have some things to learn about public speaking. Which way is best for delivering a speech?"

Types of Delivery

Jannelle's question is a good one. The correct approach to delivery can make or break a speaker. Many a boring topic or poorly developed speech has come alive for an audience in the hands of a public speaker with high-quality delivery skills. By contrast, a well researched and stimulating speech may fall flat as a result of poor delivery. The most effective public speakers view delivery as a performance.[1] As with theatre or music performance, the delivery of a speech, which is also a performance, represents the moment in which the audience will judge the entire event.

The discussion at the student union roundtable has developed because the participants are not all preparing for the same style of delivery. Four primary delivery types are most extensively used by public speakers.

Impromptu

Impromptu speeches are unplanned, unrehearsed, and spontaneous. Reactions to being asked to give an impromptu speech generally fit into one of two extremes. On the one hand, most people recoil at the thought

---

1. Ward, *Speaking of the Holy*, 5–8.

of having to speak without adequate preparation. Sometimes a professor asks for a spontaneous evaluation of a colleague's speech, or a Sunday school teacher seeks an update on the semester from a student who has returned home for the holidays. In these and similar situations, the typical reaction may be stuttering, stammering, and turning red from embarrassment. Such a moment is often followed hours later by thoughts like, "I wish I had thought to say . . . "

Others seem to enjoy the challenge of the impromptu. Their glib style makes impromptu the most inviting of all public speaking styles. In fact, occasionally a student speaker enjoys impromptu speaking to such an extent that he or she will attempt an impromptu delivery of a speech for which ample time and direction has been given to prepare. Such an approach is never an effective plan of action for those who are interested in maximizing their speaking effectiveness, or their grade point average.

For those occasions, however, when an impromptu speech is unavoidable, a few simple steps will maximize performance.

Plan Ahead

"Well-planned impromptu speeches" is not the oxymoron that it first appears. Instead some circumstances strongly indicate the possibility of an impromptu speech. Planning for such moments is wise.

Tom applied for the student assistant position in the Dean of the Chapel office on his campus. The advertising for the position indicated that a requirement included an effective Christian witness. Anticipating the interview, Tom planned a brief testimony speech, to be delivered before the interview team. When the question was asked, Tom delivered what appeared to be an impromptu speech.

Similarly, Rhonda intended to travel home for an important meeting at her local church concerning the hiring of a minister for young adults. She felt strongly about the need to create such a position. On the way to the meeting, she carefully planned what she would say in the event she was called upon.

In these and similar situations, not to plan for the unexpected is at the very least foolish and may prove disastrous. Common sense often indicates the need to prepare for impromptu speeches.

Reframe the Alternatives

In one public speaking class, impromptu speeches involved a graded assignment. Students drew a question from an envelope and were asked to speak about the question for a minimum of two minutes. Presumably the questions involved opinions and related to everyone. Nevertheless Tammy shuddered when she drew "What is your favorite movie and why?" Tammy had grown up in a strict Holiness home where movies were forbidden. Tammy quickly recovered and spoke for the allotted time on why she could not relate to the question and how she felt about her family background. She concluded her speech by declaring, "And so you see I have no favorite movie to tell you about." Tammy had effectively reframed the alternatives.

Reframing alternatives is a communication technique whereby a speaker addresses a different but related subject from the one that the audience anticipates. Reframing is common in interpersonal communication, but as Tammy demonstrated, the approach can also help a speaker out of a tight impromptu spot. Care must be taken to relate the reframe as nearly as possible to the topic at hand.

Develop General Interests

The best impromptu speakers are those that have developed a wide range of general interests. Such speakers rarely are left without some insight on the topic at hand. The development of general interests usually grows through keeping abreast of current events, keeping up with developments in one's own profession, reading widely, and maintaining friendships with a variety of people.

Memorization

The second style of delivery, the one Cynthia from the student union roundtable apparently intends to employ, is *memorization*. When delivering memorized speeches, the speaker delivers the speech word for word after committing it to memory during preparation.

In ancient Roman oratory memorized speeches were the most common. In modern times, however, there is little call for memorized speeches. Exceptions occur when very precise data is included in the speech. In addition, in certain competitions or speech contests this style may prove advantageous.

Beginning speakers sometimes attempt a memorized style believing it will minimize anxiety and thereby improve effectiveness. In fact, the opposite effect usually accompanies memorized speeches. Speakers' anxiety increases because now they have the added burden of "What if I forget?" In addition, effectiveness declines as the speaker utilizes more energy for recalling than for employing a passionate delivery. Memorized speeches are simply difficult to deliver with feeling.

In addition to these strong disadvantages, one overriding concern keeps most experienced speakers from attempting a memorized delivery. That disadvantage is time. Most speakers simply find memorization far too time consuming to employ on a regular basis.

Manuscript

One of the reasons that memorized speeches require a great deal more time for preparation is because prior to memorizing the speaker must prepare a *manuscript*. Once that manuscript has been prepared speakers often succumb to the temptation of simply using a manuscript style of delivery.

Manuscript speaking involves reading the speech from a word-for-word text. Executives or politicians sometimes use the manuscript style because they must speak several times a day and on a variety of topics. Often they have the benefit of a teleprompter to help overcome the limitations of the manuscript style. Other speakers may use a manuscript when precise words and a written record are required.

Most speakers, however, find it difficult to deliver a manuscript speech with effective feeling and emotion. In addition, the nonverbal aspects of the delivery are usually sacrificed when a manuscript is employed.

When a manuscript must be used and a teleprompter is unavailable, the best speakers type out the manuscript in double or even triple space format. They read over the manuscript numerous times, often using an underlining or highlighting technique to remind themselves of words or phrases that they intend to emphasize. Some manuscript speakers even use various color highlighters in order to indicate places for various gestures or movements from the lectern.

Such concerted efforts to camouflage the manuscript serve to point to the basic truth that manuscript speaking is not the most effective style in typical speaking situations. That distinction is reserved for the fourth and final delivery style.

Extemporaneous

Extemporaneous speeches are well-prepared speeches that are not written out or memorized. Sometimes the speaker uses a few notes or a brief presentation outline. On other occasions the speaker has so carefully rehearsed the speech that written prompts are not necessary.

Advantages of extemporaneous delivery include conveying sincerity, credibility, and confidence. One farmer, whose pastor delivered extemporaneous sermons, commented, "I like the style. When I talk about farming with a neighbor, we don't write out our comments or memorize them. We know what we're talking about. That's the same impression I get listening to the pastor's sermons."

One of the most effective political orators of all time was Winston Churchill, the Prime Minister of England during World War II. Churchill was an accomplished expository speaker. His biographer notes that he began as a combination manuscript and memorization speaker but quickly recognized the advantages of exposition and adjusted. During the move to an extemporaneous style, "Churchill had of course prepared it most carefully and more or less learned it by heart. This was not unusual in a maiden speaker of energy and ambition. What was unusual in Churchill however was that it was a practice that he continued for years to come; indeed the meticulous preparation although not the learning by heart persisted throughout the whole of his career."[2]

One of the advantages to extemporaneous delivery is the ability of the speaker to adapt. When Suzette saw raised eyebrows during her speech to inform she knew that she had failed to communicate a point effectively. Because she had prepared an extemporaneous delivery, she could say the same thing a slightly different way and help her audience understand. Will also used the extemporaneous style. As a result, he found it relatively easy to adjust to the comments of the one who introduced him to speak. With a memorized or manuscript style, such adjustments prove difficult or impossible.

Because of its effectiveness, the extemporaneous style of delivery is by far the most common in modern American culture. As a result, most speech classes require several extemporaneously delivered speeches. The balance of this chapter will therefore focus on this important style of delivery.

The Dos of Effective Delivery

The most accomplished public speakers recognize and utilize five key dos of effective delivery. These include:

- Practice the Presentation
- Be Conversational

---

2. Jenkins, *Churchill*, 72.

- Dress Appropriately
- Maintain Eye Contact
- Gesture Naturally

Practice the Presentation

Imagine an actor or actress accepting a role in a community play or other theatre production, but refusing to attend rehearsal. The performer says, "I'll learn my lines and be there on the night of the performance, but the rest of the cast will just have to practice without me." Such a performer would never become a star.

Similarly, since public speaking is a performance, the speaker who refuses to practice will never excel. The most effective public speakers practice their speeches prior to delivery. Some hold delivery practice before a mirror. Others use a video or audio tape recording. Still others gather a small audience of friends to serve as a focus group for the performance of the speech. Regardless of the format, even the most experienced speakers benefit from several out-loud dress rehearsals of the speech.

An added benefit is the fact that these practice sessions serve to minimize the communication apprehension experienced by most speakers. Much of that anxiety is actually fear of the unknown stemming from wondering, "How will this speech come out?" The well-rehearsed extemporaneous speaker knows the answer to that question. It will "come out" as it has during the several previous practice sessions.

This minimization of anxiety allows the speaker to project the kind of confidence that is crucial to public speaking success. Nervous speakers tend to fidget, sway, or shuffle.[3] In addition they avoid eye contact and may speak too rapidly or too softly. When these problems are practiced away, the audience forgets the speaker, focusing instead on the speaker's message.

Be Conversational

Jackson's speech to inform seemed wooden and stiff. His instructor suspected that Jackson had attempted to memorize the speech and had gotten the anticipated results. Jackson insisted, however, that he had not memorized. He believed that he had practiced the speech too much. Whether it is possible to over practice a speech is a debatable topic even among some speech professionals. There is consensus, however, on the fact that the final product should be natural and conversational.

3. Mulac and Sherman, "Behavioral Assessment of Speech Anxiety," 134–43.

In interpersonal conversation a participant usually does not call attention to him/herself, but to the points being made.[4] Similarly, the effective speaker will be natural or conversational to such an extent that the audience focuses on the speech, not the speaker.

This *conversational style* is very similar to that employed by an individual engaged in a one-on-one conversation about a topic that he or she feels passionate about. There is no pausing to reflect on what should be said next. There is no quiet reservation. Neither is there an over dramatization of the delivery. Instead, in such conversation, lively and animated speaking is the norm. Gestures support the words. The conversationalist may move slightly to the right or to the left in order to gain a better vantage from which to deliver a point. Such are the characteristics of the conversationally delivered speech.

> *Conversational style*: Speech delivery style where the speaker appears to be engaged in a one-on-one conversation with the audience.

Dress Appropriately

Americans place a high premium on physical appearance. Millions of dollars are poured annually into the purchase of cosmetics, hair care products, diet aids, and designer clothes. In recent years purchasers have trended toward spending those dollars on a more laid-back look. Comfort and casualness have replaced propriety and formality in modern American styles.

Meanwhile, studies continue to demonstrate that appearance influences the perception that others have of an individual. Americans think of those who are attractive as credible, happy, popular, and prosperous when compared to less attractive counterparts.[5] In addition, it has been demonstrated that attractive students receive higher grades, are more persuasive, and are more likely to get a job.[6]

Similarly, what an instructor wears to the classroom has impact on students' perception.[7] Research has found that students associate attire with a teacher's attitude, credibility, and approachability.

---

4. McCrowsky, *An Introduction To Rhetorical Communication*, 249.
5. Beebe et al., Communication, 188.
6. Richmond and McCroskey, *Nonverbal Behavior in Interpersonal Relations*, 25.
7. Gorham and Cohen, "Fashion in the Classroom III," 281–99.

Other studies have found a close correlation between clothing and response to an individual. By means of clothing alone, observers believe that they can determine a person's economic, educational, and social background.[8] Even more important to a public speaker's credibility is the fact that observers declare that clothing serves as a measure of trustworthiness, successfulness, and moral character.

One team of researchers specifically noted that the addition of a jacket to a female's skirt and blouse outfit caused participants to rate the subject as more powerful.[9] Other experts have similarly concluded that a man's business suit sends messages of authority and credibility.[10]

In response to these and similar studies and to the demands of customers and clients many firms are tightening their employee dress codes.[11] Those changes simply make good economic sense for businesses from department stores to investment firms to health clubs. Those firms recognize that none of this data speaks to the rightness or wrongness of the high correlation between appearance and audience perception. That correlation is simply a fact. Effective public speakers acknowledge that fact and use it to gain a speaking advantage.

Precise dress codes for speaking in class will depend upon the individual instructor, the audience analysis completed by the speaker, and even the thesis statement for the particular speech. A few general guidelines, however, will prove helpful in almost every situation.

1. Baseball caps or other headwear worn indoors constitutes a breach of etiquette; this is especially noticeable when the wearer is speaking to a group.
2. T-shirts with printed messages may alter the audience's perception of the verbal message.
3. Professional appearance increases speaker credibility.
4. Immodest apparel draws the audience attention away from the message.

With these truths in mind, the effective speaker dresses appropriately for the speech.

---

8. Thourlby, *You Are What You Wear*, 23.
9. Temple and Loewen, "Perceptions of Power," 339–48.
10. Richmond and McCroskey, *Nonverbal Behavior in Interpersonal Relations*, 240.
11. Irvine, "Dress Codes Get Back To Business."

Maintain Eye Contact

In North American culture eye contact is seen as evidence of trustworthiness and integrity. The inability or unwillingness to maintain eye contact may signal disinterest or unfriendliness. No wonder at least one public speaking expert believes that "the single most important physical action in public speaking is to have eye contact with the audience."[12]

That explains why the most effective speakers scan the audience, looking various audience members in the eye on a random basis. These speakers avoid limiting their gaze to the first one or two rows. They also refuse to single out special friends or prominent people in the audience. Instead they give the appearance through eye contact of speaking directly and personally to every person in the audience.

When Jamie watched the videotape of her first speech, she was surprised and distraught at how little eye contact she maintained. Jamie realized that she spent a great deal of time looking down at the extensive presentation outline she had carried with her to the podium. Upon reflection Jamie recognized that she probably had not needed so many notes, and she certainly had not needed to refer to them so frequently. Jamie had learned the valuable public speaking principle that notes and manuscripts are the enemy of eye contact. The more printed words a speaker carries to the speaking assignment, the more those words will be relied upon. Effective speakers minimize notes and thus maximize eye contact.

Gesture Naturally

In addition to maintaining eye contact, the most effective public speakers *gesture* frequently and naturally. Gestures are those hand and body movements that accompany a speech. Candidly observing an interpersonal conversation in process reveals that most people talk with their hands as well as their words. Conversational style includes gesturing.

Some time ago, nonverbal communication experts, Ekman and Friesen separated gestures into three categories.[13]

- Emblems
- Illustrators
- Adaptors

Their landmark work continues to influence the study of gesturing today.

---

12. Axtell, *Do's and Taboos of Public Speaking*, 67.
13. Ekman and Friesen, "The Repertoire of Nonverbal Behavior," 49–98.

Emblems are gestures that stand for or take the place of a word. For example, a nod of the head means yes, while a shake of the head means no. Anxiety caused Eileen to speak so softly during her first speech that her instructor could not even hear her. When Dr. Fields put a hand behind his ear, he communicated with Eileen via an emblem without interrupting her speech.

> *Emblems:* Gestures that stand for or take the place of a word.

Illustrators are gestures that add emphasis to words but do not replace the words. Illustrators are the most common form of speech gesture. As Calvin gave his speech to inform on the nation of Uganda, he referred to the map that he had projected as a visual aid. "It is in this northwest region of the country that most of the Sudanese refugees have arrived," he said. Calvin's point to the map was an illustrator. Similarly, Jeanne used an illustrator when she moved her arm in an extended arch slowly across the audience as she said, "We should all be regular chapel attendees."

> *Illustrators:* Gestures that add emphasis to words but do not replace the words.

Adaptors are gestures that demonstrate stress or fear. As such they should usually be avoided by a public speaker. Mike repeatedly tapped on the lectern with the pencil he held in his hand during his speech. Sherrie tugged at a stray strand of hair as she spoke. Danielle used her thumb to twist the diamond on her ring finger as she presented her speech to inform. In each case the adaptors demonstrated the stress of the speaker and distracted the audience.

> *Adaptors:* Gestures that demonstrate stress or fear.

And Don'ts

In addition to these five dos for effective delivery, five don'ts will enhance the performance of any speaker when carefully followed. The delivery don'ts are:

- Chew Gum
- Use Slang or Jargon
- Emulate a Fig Leaf
- Use Filler Words
- Create Motion Sickness

Don't Chew Gum

Gum chewing makes it difficult to speak clearly and distinctly. In addition, the facial movements associated with chewing distracts an attentive audience. Effective speakers, therefore, never attempt to chew gum or eat during their speech.

Don't Use Slang or Jargon

Slang is language outside conventional or standard usage that has a new or extended meaning. In most cases slang should be avoided in public speaking because not every audience member will understand the slang term. In a speech to inform entitled "Creating the Perfect First Date," Josh said, "No girl wants to feel like she has been hit on." Most of the people in Josh's audience understood the slang term "hit on" to refer to being propositioned in a sexual manner. Josh's audience included an international student who had never heard the slang expression before. He admitted later to being perplexed about how beating on a young lady with one's fists fit the context of the speech. Such misunderstandings usually accompany the use of slang.

Careful speakers also avoid the use of *jargon*. Jargon is the specialized vocabulary of those in the same work or way of life. Carefully defining terms for an audience helps avoid the misunderstandings that easily arise from the use of such specialized terms.

Don't Emulate a Fig Leaf

Beginning speakers often struggle over what to do with their hands. One of the most common, but least effective, solutions is to fold the hands one over the other just below the waist. Experts refer to such a pose as the "fig leaf" stance. The fig leaf stance communicates apprehension, and the need to cover one's most vulnerable areas. Polished speakers avoid such a posture. Instead they practice their speech until they can use their hands in effective gesturing.

Don't Use Filler Words

Twenty-first century Americans live in a noisy world and have very little experience with silence. As a result, most moderns feel very uncomfortable when confronted with the absence of noise. This discomfort is intensified when one stands before a group of people, who seem to hold him or her personally responsible for the quiet. Such is the plight of the modern speaker. Every pause, whether for breath or to collect thoughts, causes the speaker to feel uncomfortable and threatened. The natural tendency is to avoid such pauses at all costs. Instead, the speaker tries to fill the silence with unintelligible guttural sounds or meaningless words. Such noises are called filler words or *vocalized pauses*.

> *Vocalized pause*: Unintelligible guttural sounds or meaningless word designed to fill the silence caused by natural pauses.

The most common filler words are *uh*, *um*, and *and*. In a four minute and thirty-four second speech, one student counted twenty-six *um*s as he viewed the videotape of a speech to inform. Such frequency distracts an audience and minimizes the speaker's effectiveness.

Curt discovered the tendency to use the word *and* as a filler word in his speeches. Overuse of the conjunction has the multiple effects of a distracting filler and the creation of a long compound sentence.

Other speakers have created filler words by misusing expressions and terms. *Like* became a filler word in Fran's speech when she used the word frequently and improperly. The word *like* has a definite meaning in purpose in the English language. *Like* establishes a comparison between two entities by referring to them as being the same or having similar qualities. For example, "The older boy was dressed like his younger brother," establishes a similarity between the two youngsters with regard to their attire. In her speech Fran said, "Like, I went to the student center immediately after chapel, but, like, the rest of the group was, like, already gone." No similarities are established in Fran's sentence. Fran has merely created a distracting filler word.

Don't Create Motion Sickness

Joyce watched a videotape of her speech of self-introduction and completed the assigned self-evaluation. Among the comments she wrote, "I got motion sick watching myself rock from side to side throughout the speech."

Joyce's observation is not unique. The anxiety that arises from public speaking creates adrenaline. Often working off that adrenaline produces rocking, repetitive, or other unnatural motions. Such motion, while not literally leading to motion sickness, does indeed distract audience members.

Simply observing the problem in that first speech helped Joyce to perform much better on her next speech assignment. Often beginning speakers discover that distracting motions, like distracting expressions, are easily eliminated with heightened awareness.

The Chapter in Brief

Public speaking is a performance, and as such it requires diligent practice in order to maximize effectiveness. The style of delivery chosen by the speaker will also make a great deal of difference in the end result. Four primary styles of delivery include:

- Impromptu
- Memorized
- Manuscript
- Extemporaneous

For many occasions, the well-prepared extemporaneous speech is the most effective. The performance of a speech in this style is enhanced by using five dos and five don'ts of speech delivery.

Do:
- Practice the Presentation
- Be Conversational
- Dress Appropriately
- Maintain Eye Contact
- Gesture Naturally

Don't:
- Chew Gum
- Use Slang or Jargon
- Emulate a Fig Leaf
- Use Filler Words
- Create Motion Sickness

Key Terms

Use the list below to test your knowledge of the vocabulary introduced in this chapter.

- impromptu speeches
- memorized speeches
- manuscript speeches
- extemporaneous speeches
- conversational style
- reframing the alternatives
- gestures
- emblems
- illustrators
- adaptors
- slang
- jargon
- filler words

For Review and Discussion

1. Consider the four primary delivery styles introduced in this chapter. What are the advantages of each style? What are the disadvantages of each?

2. One student argued, "How a person dresses is a personal matter. An audience should not reject a speaker's ideas on such a shallow basis." How do you respond?

3. What are the differences between public speaking and conversation? In what ways are they similar? Why is conversational style so effective?

4. Think of a public speaker that has impressed you in the past. What style of delivery did that speaker use? What evidences did you see of the five dos and the five don'ts presented in this chapter?

Proclamation Practice

Develop a two-to-three minute speech of edification for a class devotional. Videotape the delivery of the speech, and then watch and compare your performance to the lists of dos and don'ts from this chapter.

9

Speeches to Inform

Chapter Challenges

A careful reading of Chapter 9 will provide insight into these chapter challenges:

1. Identify the purpose of a speech to inform.
2. What are three possible approaches to a speech to inform?
3. What organizational structures are typically used in a speech to inform? Describe how to properly use each structure.
4. What seven public speaking tips should be applied to the speech to inform?

At the Student Union Roundtable

"Remember we only have until the end of the week to turn in our speech to inform topic to Dr. Connelly," reminded Ryan as the public speaking study group gathered at the student union roundtable. "Who has decided on a topic?"

"I want to inform the class on my native Honduras," offered Belsa. "My title for the speech will be 'Understanding the Government, Culture, and History of Honduras.'"

"It sounds interesting," encouraged Cynthia.

"And no doubt about your credibility on the subject," Jannelle added.

Jess frowned. "But don't forget that this is only a five to seven minute speech. I seriously doubt if you can cover that topic in such a short time."

Cynthia nodded. "Dr. Connelly did say it was sometimes hard to limit the topic appropriately."

"I guess you're right," Belsa reluctantly agreed. "I'll keep working on it."

"I have another kind of problem with my topic," said Janelle. "I want to do my speech on the preparations necessary for a short-term missions trip. I'm sure I can limit that to five to seven minutes, but I may be too excited about the topic.

"How can you be too excited about a topic?" asked Ryan.

Janelle responded, "Well, I went on my first trip last summer. It was a life-changing experience for me. I honestly think that everyone should go on a one or two week mission trip. I don't know how to keep the speech just informative and not let it become a speech to persuade."

Informative Speaking

Janelle's concern is a valid one. In one sense all public speaking is persuasive, since speakers do not usually choose topics on which they have no opinion or feel no passion. The difference between a *speech to inform* and a speech to persuade lies in the fact that a speech to persuade has a clear call to action. On the other hand, the speech to inform is limited to telling the audience something that the speaker believes they will find interesting or beneficial. Informing is sharing knowledge, and thus informative speakers seek to educate their audience.

> *Speech to inform*: Speech about objects, people, events, processes, concepts, or issues designed to enhance an audience member's knowledge or understanding.

Informative speeches may be speeches about objects, people, events, processes, concepts, or issues. In each case the speaker presents information designed to enhance an audience member's knowledge or understanding.

Informative speaking is an important part of everyday life in America. The present time has been labeled "the information age." That is because more information has been published in the last thirty years than in the previous five thousand. It has been estimated that the available information is doubling every two and a half years.[1] This tremendous volume of information may explain why recent graduates, when they were ask to rank the speech skill that they find most important in their jobs, listed informative speaking as number one.[2]. Nearly two-thirds of the respondents in another survey said they used informative speaking almost constantly in their work.[3]

Speech to Inform Purposes

Engleberg suggests that the speech to inform is designed to accomplish one or more of three purposes.[4]

Provide New Information

First, the speech may serve the purpose of providing new information. When this is the case, the speaker will include the basic who, what, when, where, and how of the topic. In addition, the speaker will need to take great care to define terms which may be unfamiliar to the audience.

James had grown up in a third world country where his parents were missionaries. As a result, he was the only member of his speech class that had ever attended a boarding school. Therefore his speech to inform, entitled "Life in a Boarding School," was new information for the members of his audience.

---

1. Banach, "Are You Too Busy to Think?" 351–53.
2. Johnson and Szczupakiewicz, "The Public Speaking Course," 131–37.
3. Wolvin and Corley, "The Technical Speech Communication Course," 83–91.
4. Engleberg, *The Principles of Public Presentation*, 274

Enhance Information

A second possible purpose of a speech to inform is to enhance information. In this speech the emphasis is on supplemental or recently released data. The speaker will need to dig deeper for information in preparing for this speech. The speaker will also usually need to explore the topic from several different angles.

Billy gave his speech to inform on "The James Ossuary." Many in the class had read of the discovery of the ossuary purported to have been the final resting-place of James the brother of Jesus, but since Billy had interviewed Dr. Ben Witherington, an expert on antiquity relics, he was able to provide enhanced information on the subject.

Clarify Information

The third purpose of a speech to inform involves clarifying information. Here the speaker may need to focus upon the task of countering misinformation, which is sometimes a very difficult assignment. Credibility will be especially important to the speaker delivering this type of informative speech, since audience members have already formed an opinion and will need to be convinced that the speaker knows more than their previous sources.

Angela, and the others in her class had all heard the rumors circulating the campus that a new policy would be put in place in the fall semester whereby seniors would not be allowed to live on campus. According, to the rumor, the new policy was designed to free up limited housing for underclassmen. Angela however, had discussed the matter with Dean of Students, Thomas DeKnapf. Based upon that interview Angela was convinced that seniors would not be forced off campus. Instead all upperclassmen, sophomores through seniors, would be given priority in a new apartment complex that the university had purchased in another part of the city. Angela's speech, "The Truth about Campus Housing Next Fall," was a speech designed to clarify information.

Speech to Inform Approaches

As speakers strive to provide new information, enhance information, or clarify information they will usually use one of three approaches. These are:

- Demonstrate
- Describe
- Define

Speeches That Demonstrate

Demonstration speeches tell the audience how to do something or how something works. Such speeches are common in our culture and extremely practical. An advertiser demonstrates how a product works. A manufacturer demonstrates how to assemble a product. A professor demonstrates how to properly do an assignment. Each of these has delivered a demonstration speech to inform.

Pamela delivered a speech to inform to her class entitled "How to Bake Chocolate Chip Cookies." Dick's speech explored the subject "Developing an Effective Devotional Life." Brandy showed the class the correct way to wrap a gift in her speech to inform. All three of these class members used the demonstration approach.

Speeches That Describe

A *description speech* is designed to paint mental pictures of persons, places, events, activities, concepts, or objects. The use of vivid and clear language is important in a descriptive speech. The effective speaker, however, uses language that focuses on what is being described rather than drawing attention to the language itself.

When Ronald delivered his speech to inform on "Life in Uganda," he relied heavily on the descriptive approach. His first hand experience having grown up on the mission field in Uganda made the word pictures accurate as well as clear to the audience.

Speeches That Define

Some speeches to inform seek to explain or define terms, concepts, beliefs, theories, policies, or ideas. Often such a speech involves helping the audience understand the abstract. This can become more difficult and complex than other speeches to inform. As a result, definition speeches require intensive preparation for effective delivery. The more complicated the subject of the *definitional speech* to inform, the more care must be given to delivering the speech.

Some speeches to inform which have used the definitional approach include:

- What is Domestic Violence?
- The True Meaning of True Love
- Anorexia: Killer of Young Adults
- Fitness Facts

- Abortion: The Ultimate Child Abuse
- Harry Potter's Impact on Children

Speech to Inform Structures

Regardless of the approach used, the speaker must present the points of the speech in a logical order. That is accomplished by means of one of several organizational structures that exist for a speech to inform. The nature and content of the speech will determine which structure should be used for a particular speech. Five of the most common organizational structures for a speech to inform are *topical, chronological, spatial, causal* and *pro/con*.

Topical

The *topical structure* is the most common organizational structure for a speech to inform. This structure serves to narrow broad topics by dividing them into their component sub-topics. Sometimes it allows the speaker to fit limited time allotments by selecting only those topics which are most interesting to the speaker or relevant to the audience.

Jennifer gave a speech to inform on her home state of Alaska. While she could not tell all there is to tell about Alaska in five to seven minutes, she selected three sub-topics that made her speech manageable. She referred to these as myths that needed debunking. The outline was

1. The myth of Alaskan climate
2. The myth of Alaskan resources
3. The myth of Alaskan darkness

Lauren loved gardening. Her speech to inform might have followed several organizational patterns. She chose a topical structure and divided the various garden crops into sub-topics.

1. Plants that bear food
2. Plants that are food
3. Plants that are rooted by food

Dustin enjoyed a good cup of coffee. He wanted to present a speech to inform on the various types of coffee. He discovered the topic was appropriate for his audience and easy to research. His sub-topics for the speech were:

1. Dark roasts
2. Blends
3. Specialties

Many beginning speakers choose to use a topical structure because it lends itself to almost any informative topic. The second organizational structure is not quite so universal but still strongly supports a number of topics.

Chronological

The *chronological structure* organizes a speech according to a time sequence. Here the speaker relates a topic by providing the steps in the process or showing the order of the incidents. The structure is most effective for explaining procedures or stages.

Mike chose a chronological ordering for a speech to inform on how to change a flat tire. His main points were:

1. Set the brake
2. Jack the vehicle
3. Replace the tire
4. Lower the vehicle

Similarly, Evelyn used a chronological structure for her speech entitled "How to Prepare a Speech To Inform." Her main points were:

1. Select the topic
2. Research the topic
3. Organize the information
4. Practice the delivery
5. Receive the applause

Will used the chronological order for his speech on the correct way to shoot a free throw in basketball. He carefully explained each of these main points.

1. Step to the line
2. Eye the target
3. Release the ball
4. Follow-through

Sandra utilized a simple three-step approach to taking good class notes. Her material, presented in a speech to inform, best fit the chronological structure.

1. Before the lecture
2. During the lecture
3. After the lecture

Spatial

Another useful structure for many speeches to inform is the *spatial* ordering of points. This structure is most useful for those speeches that are concerned with the physical or geographic characteristics of a place or thing. It is also the structure most common for describing the parts of a whole.

Jenny's speech entitled, "A Tour of the University Library" used a spatial ordering. Her main points were

1. Reference and Reserve on Main Floor
2. Periodicals in the Basement
3. Stacks on the Second and Third Floors

Nathan also used the spatial ordering for his speech to inform on the best golf courses in the State of Indiana. His two-point speech followed the outline:

1. Best Courses in the Indianapolis area
2. Best Courses in Rural Areas

Causal

The *causal* or cause-effect structure is frequently used for persuasive speeches but is also an appropriate structure for a speech to inform. The inverse of the structure, effect to cause, is also sometimes used.

Lee used the causal structure to discuss cardiovascular health in his speech to inform. Lee's outline reflected three primary causes of poor cardiovascular health.

1. Lack of Exercise
2. Obesity
3. Fatty Foods

Roland also used the causal structure for his speech to inform. His title was "Small Business Failure." He listed several causes for such failures as his main points.

1. Economic Downturns
2. Strong Competition
3. Government Overregulation

Pro / Con

The *pro/con structure* is designed to present both sides of an issue. The emphasis in this structure is on balance. A similar structure, in a speech to persuade, focuses on the relative advantage of one particular course of action over another. Beginning public speakers usually discover that the pro/con structure requires more delivery time than other structures. It is important, therefore, to plan carefully and time the delivery during preparation in order to stay within required time guidelines.

Samantha used the pro/con structure effectively in her speech to inform on universal health care. Her outline demonstrates this approach.

1. Advantages of government sponsored health care
    a. Every American Covered
    b. The Concept of Justice Affirmed
2. Disadvantages of Government Sponsored Health Care
    a. Increased Cost Due to Governmental Inefficiency
    b. Loss of Personal Choice

In his speech on Christian elementary and secondary schools, Ross used the pro/con structure to explore both sides of the issue. His basic outline for the speech looked like this:

1. Advantages of Christian Schools
    a. Learn Faith Issues
    b. Improved Academic Performance
    c. Develop Christian Friendships
2. Disadvantages of Christian Schools
    a. Abandon the Lost
    b. Increased Costs to Parents
    c. Graduates Lack Experience With Diverse Populations

Speech to Inform Tips

A well-prepared and well-delivered speech to inform uses all of the principles for speeches in general. In addition, careful attention to a series of guidelines especially for speeches to inform will make this special category of speeches effective and memorable. These seven guidelines are offered below as "info-tips."

Info-Tip #1 Be Accurate

Information offered in a speech to inform must be accurate. Inaccuracies in a speech may seriously impact the credibility of the speaker. Audiences assume that if the speaker is wrong about one point, then there may be other inaccuracies in the speech. From that beginning point it is a short step to assuming that the speaker is not credible enough to be taken seriously.

In a pro/con speech to inform on the issue of gun control, Grayson consistently referred to the right to keep and bear arms as the Third Amendment right. Many in the audience knew that it was the Second Amendment, which guaranteed that right. Grayson's credibility was damaged because he failed to be accurate.

In addition to the problem of credibility, inaccurate information has the potential to harm an audience member who relies on that information. In some cases this misinformation can be very serious or even deadly.

For example, when Kylie gave her speech to inform on the new mall located on the far side of the city, she included directions from the campus. If audience members had followed the directions precisely, they would have turned against traffic onto a one-way street. Kylie's inaccuracies had the potential to bring serious harm to an audience member.

Info-Tip #2 Be Precise

The effective speech to inform should be clear and to the point. Audiences are turned off by information overload. It is true that precision in language and in speech development is sometimes difficult to achieve. But it is also true that the results are worth the extra effort because of the lasting impact of the speech.

Brian gave a speech to inform on AIDS. He topically arranged the speech around two points. These were the development of the disease and the devastating impact of the disease. Since Brian had visited the continent of Africa during a recent spring break mission trip, he also made a strong appeal on the need for a cure. That information was accurate and Brian's credibility was high. Yet he needed to be more precise by staying to his stated thesis in order to make the speech to inform most effective. In fact, in this case Brian's deviation from his thesis actually made his speech more persuasive than informational.

Brenda gave an excellent speech to inform on the history of the piano. In a sort of pre-introduction statement she noted how long she had been playing the piano, how lessons had helped her, and why she believed the instrument to be so important to the culture in general, even though these points had nothing to do with the history of the instrument. Brenda's audience became confused about the real reason for her speech because she failed to get to the point. In addition, Brenda's slow start created a significant time problem on the speech assignment.

Info-Tip #3 Be Relevant

As an amateur photographer who developed her own photographs, Jessica planned to do a chronologically ordered speech on setting up your own dark room. Her research, however, uncovered a fabulous book on interior design with ideas for space utilization. Since she had no clear thesis statement, Jessica got bogged down in her research and added several paragraphs of irrelevant information on how to free up the space for a dark room at home.

Every aspect of a speech to inform should relate to the audience and to the main purpose of the speech. The importance of relevance to an audience can best be seen in a classroom where the instructor gives advance notice of topics that will or will not be on an upcoming exam. "This will be on the test," makes the information immediately relevant to the students. As a result attention is heightened, and the classroom audience is involved in the communication process. By contrast, "This will not be on the test" has exactly the opposite impact.

Good informative speakers search for ways to make their speech relevant to their audience.[5] Some speakers have increased the relevance of their speech by:

- Using examples that are relevant
- Using participatory exercises that involve the audience
- Using explanations that demonstrate relevance
- Using personal experiences
- Using current events as illustrations

Info-Tip #4 Be Creative

The informative speech, more than any other type of speech, requires the speaker to find creative approaches in order to keep the attention of the audience. Vivid language is a vital way to be creative in the speech to inform. The language selected should help the audience use all of their five senses in experiencing the speech. Audiences should not just hear the speech, but because of word choices, they should feel it, smell it, taste it, and touch it as well.

Humor is another important creative tool in an informative speaker's toolbox. Research demonstrates that humor serves to lighten the mood and make audience members more receptive.[6] It is important, however, that

---

5. Frymier and Shulman, "What's In It For Me?" 40–50.
6. Wanzer and Frymier, "The Relationship," 48–62.

the humor match the audience's idea of what is funny.[7] Further, humor should never belittle or make fun of other individuals or people groups.[8]

Info-Tip #5 Be Supported

Each point in a speech to inform must be adequately supported by research. Support may come in the form of data from studies, quotes from experts, or personal experience. In every case an audience member must be able to clearly conclude that the positions presented in the speech are supported by the facts.

Simon had been taught as a child in Sunday school that the author of the biblical book of James was not the brother of Jesus. But as he developed his speech to inform on the topic of the authors of the various New Testament books, he discovered that position could not be supported. Both external evidence and the highly refined Greek included in the book supported the more traditional authorship. Simon had to adjust his position in favor of one more clearly supportable.

Courtney planned a speech to inform on the appropriateness of "right to die" legislation. She felt strongly about the topic, since her own grandmother had recently endured many months of painful illness prior to her death. After doing research, however, Courtney decided that "right to die" did not really fit within her understanding of a Christian worldview, which emphasized the value of all human life. Courtney changed topics rather than develop a speech on a topic where her personal point of view could not be adequately supported.

Info-Tip #6 Be Logical

To be most effective the speech to inform should use the appropriate structure and a logical progression. When done correctly, the audience anticipates the points because of the logical progression of ideas.

Caitlyn's speech to inform on wars involving the United States during the twentieth century began with the Gulf War. She then discussed World War I, as well as Vietnam and Korea, before ending the speech with a discussion of the Second World War. A more logical structure would follow chronology either from most recent to first, or first to last.

In a speech to inform called "A Tour of the People's House," Stacy attempted a verbal and photographic tour of the governor's mansion. Since a spatial order is the most logical for such a speech, Stacy's audience became

---

7. Gruner, "Advice to the Beginning Speaker," 142–47.
8. Smith and Power, "The Use of Disparaging Humor," 279–92.

a bit confused when she began with renovations to the structure, using a chronological format.

Info-Tip #7 Be Participatory

Arguably the most important of the seven info-tips is to be participatory. The audience must become involved in the speech if it is to become effective and memorable. Sometimes audience participation is accomplished through one or more rhetorical questions. At other times a handout where the audience follows along in a "how to" speech accomplishes the participatory need. On other occasions a spot survey where the audience is ask to raise their hand if they have ever had a particular experience or heard a specific term serves to invite participation.

One effective participatory technique is the *question and answer period*. While student speakers are sometimes reluctant to put themselves on the spot, the question and answer period can be used very effectively to encourage audience involvement in the speech. In a small audience, speakers sometimes choose to encourage questions at any time during the speech. Most speakers, especially in larger audiences, are more comfortable adding a question and answer period at the end of the speech. Those who do add a question and answer period to their speech to inform will benefit from following four important rules for handling such situations.

> *Question / Answer period*: A participatory technique that allows audience members to clarify their understanding of a point or points in the speech.

Rule #1 Preparation is Still the Key

A question and answer period does not forgo the need to prepare. Asking friends to hear the practice session for a speech and then raise questions can provide advance warning of logical questions. Similarly, what a speaker leaves out of a speech can often guide an audience toward a desired question. Some speakers anticipate the most difficult of all possible questions.[9] Being prepared to answer these tough questions makes the typical questions quite simple.

---

9. Maher, "Career Journal."

Rule #2 Answer in a Straightforward Manner

The Biblical injunction "Simply let your 'yes' be 'yes,' and your 'no,' 'no'"[10] should be especially applied to the question and answer period. A question should never be viewed as a springboard for a new speech or the pursuit of a side topic.

Rule #3 Don't Allow Questioners to Take Over

The speaker is ultimately responsible for the time and development of the speech. Allowing audience participation is not an invitation to yield the floor to an audience member. Sometimes the speaker will need to hurry a questioner along or insist on discussing a matter after the public assembly has ended in order to prevent a questioner take-over.

Rule #4 Never become angry or defensive

In spite of the best efforts of a speaker, some questioners will see the question and answer time as an opportunity for rebuttal or to take pot shots at the speech. Yielding to anger in such a situation gives the questioner much more control than the speaker should allow.

The Chapter in Brief

Speeches to inform are among the most common and important in American culture. Every speech to inform will either provide new information, enhance information, or it will clarify information. Three approaches to informative speaking are used to accomplish these purposes. Each speech will demonstrate, describe, or define.

Common structures for speeches to inform are

- Topical
- Chronological
- Spatial
- Causal
- Pro/Con

A series of tips for preparing and delivering a speech to inform will help assure the speaker's success. The seven info-tips are

- Be Accurate
- Be Precise
- Be Relevant

---

10. Matthew 5:37 NIV.

- Be Creative
- Be Supported
- Be Logical
- Be Participatory

Key Terms

Use the list below to test your knowledge of the vocabulary introduced in this chapter.

- speech to inform
- pro-con structure
- definitional speech
- demonstration speech
- topical structure
- chronological structure
- spatial structure
- description speech
- causal structure

For Review and Discussion

1. At the student union roundtable, Janelle raised the issue of the difference between a speech to inform and a speech to persuade. In light of this chapter how do you see that difference?
2. Listed below are some topics for in-class speeches to inform. In each case decide whether the speech would be demonstrating, describing, or defining. Then select the organizational structure that you believe would be best for that speech.
   - How to toss a salad
   - How to perform CPR
   - The functions of the internal combustion engine
   - George W. Bush's early years
   - Capital punishment and the Bible
   - How to memorize Scripture
   - The terrorist threat
   - African delicacies
   - Developing an exercise program
   - A tour of the Eiffel Tower
   - Understanding anorexia
   - How the Federal Reserve controls inflation

- The history of basketball
- Caring for a goldfish
- Is a Christian college for you?
- How to build a bookcase
- Playing the flute
- The life of the Apostle Paul
- My favorite author

Proclamation Practice

Prepare for delivery to the class a five to seven minute speech to inform on a topic of your choice. End the speech with a brief question and answer period.

10

Speeches to Persuade

Chapter Challenges

A careful reading of Chapter 10 will provide insights into these chapter challenges:

1. Define persuasion.
2. What are the four elements of persuasion?
3. Describe three principles of persuasion.
4. Explain the difference between statements of fact, value, and policy.

5. What are three typical organizational structures for persuasive speeches?
6. Name and describe three persuasive appeals.

At the Student Union Roundtable

"Since all advertising is persuasive, I think I'll simply select a product and persuade the audience to buy," offered Jannelle as the public speaking study group met at the student union roundtable. "What are some of the rest of you choosing for a speech to persuade topic?"

"I intend to build off the research I already did for the speech to inform," Belsa responded. "My topic this time will be 'Why you should visit Honduras.'"

"My mother is an investment advisor," Jess offered. "She's sending me some material that I can use to persuade the class to begin a savings and investment program early."

"I'm struggling with the right topic for this assignment," admitted Ryan. "Originally I planned to do a speech persuading the class that capital punishment is an appropriate and God-authorized punishment for certain crimes. I did a survey of the class as part of my audience analysis and discovered that 80 percent of the class already agrees with that position."

"It sounds like they are already persuaded," Jess said.

"That's my problem. How do you persuade people who already agree with your premise? Maybe I'll have to change to persuading the class that the earth is flat." Ryan continued with a grin.

Persuasion Defined

Ryan has expressed a common misunderstanding about persuasion and the role of a persuader in public speaking. Sometimes speakers view persuasion like two sides of a coin. Persuasion, they reason, only occurs when the audience is moved from heads to tails on a given topic. That view assumes that every issue has only two possible points of view.

But of course, every issue is not black or white, yes or no, heads or tails. In fact, for most topics an entire continuum of positions exists. A speaker's position may be at any point along that continuum, while any individual audience member may hold a different position along the same continuum. The persuasive task becomes to move the audience closer to the speaker's position.

Sometimes both the speaker and the audience tend toward the same position. The speaker will thus need to adopt a *reinforcement strategy* in order to strengthen or reinforce the audience position. A reinforcement strategy is used when the audience and the speaker are in basic agreement.

> *Reinforcement strategy*: Strategy of persuasion designed to strengthen an audience's position when the audience and speaker are in basic agreement.

When Camille presented a speech to persuade on the right to life, she discovered through her audience analysis that her audience was nearly unanimously in agreement with her position that abortion is morally wrong. She reinforced that point of view and encouraged the audience to alter their behavior by supporting organizations which offer adoption as an alternative.

In other cases an audience member or the entire audience may be much closer to the position at the opposite end of the continuum from that of the speaker. As a result, the speaker will need to adopt a *reversal strategy*. This strategy seeks to reverse the audience position and bring them to the point of view of the speaker

> *Reversal strategy*: Persuasion strategy adopted by the speaker when the audience holds an initial position different than the speaker.

Dan used a reversal strategy in his attempt to convince the class to support his position to allow alcohol in the dormitories of his Christian University. He attempted to alter or reverse their attitudes and encouraged audience members to sign his petition to university administrators.

Both reinforcement and reversal fit the general definition of *persuasion*. Persuasion is the process of getting others to alter thinking on a topic. The speaker attempts to get the audience members to change their minds.[1] Usually, this change of mind leads to a change of action or behavior. Thus persuasion is the process by which a speaker attempts to elicit a voluntary change in the attitudes, beliefs, values, or behavior of another. There are three key elements in this definition.[2]

---

1. Gardner, *Changing Minds*. 1.
2. Neff, *A Pastor's Guide to Interpersonal Communication*, 166.

First, persuasion involves a process. Communication must usually occur over time for persuasion to take place. The persuasive speech is just one form of that communication.

Second, persuasion involves voluntary change. Persuasion is not the same thing as coercion. The threat or use of force is never a part of the persuasive process. The rise to power of Adolf Hitler and the Third Reich provides a remarkable example. While today he is viewed as a deranged maniac, in the earliest days of his power he fooled his own people as well as leaders around the world. In reality, before he became a ruthless, tyrannical demagogue, he was an effective persuader to whom people voluntarily acquiesced.

Third, while persuasion involves a change in attitudes, beliefs, and values, it also includes a change in behaviors. That is why every effective persuasive speech must include a call to action. The speaker must tell audience members what he or she expects of them as a result of their changed attitudes, beliefs, or values.

Elements of Persuasion

Four terms that are often used interchangeably actually have more precise definitions. A thorough understanding of the four will set the stage for effective persuasion. These four elements of persuasion are:

- Attitudes
- Beliefs
- Values
- Behaviors

Attitudes

An *attitude* is a mental position with regard to something or someone. One student may have a positive attitude toward living on campus, Democratic candidates, and the Southern Baptist Church. Her roommate has a positive attitude toward having her own apartment, Republican candidates, and the United Methodist Church.

Attitudes can rarely be expressed in absolute terms. Instead they represent varying degrees of strength and support. For example, Karly declared, "I love everything about my class on Paul's epistles. It is the best class I've ever taken." But when Angela reminded her of Dr. Meek's tests, which were notoriously difficult, she realized that her expressed attitude was not in fact complete. She still had very positive attitudes about the class, but not a totally positive attitude.

Attitudes are a mental position, but they usually precipitate actions. For example, if Brittany has a favorable attitude toward Mexican food, you would expect her to eat at the local Mexican restaurant more frequently than her counterpart with an unfavorable attitude toward that specialty cuisine.

Beliefs

A *belief* is confidence in the existence or reality of someone or something. There are similarities between beliefs and attitudes. Beliefs are really clustering of attitudes. For example, the belief that Jesus Christ is Lord will grow out of a clustering of attitudes about the person of Christ, the nature of the church, the need for redemption, and the fallen state of human beings.

Like attitudes, beliefs usually are a precursor to action. For instance, believing that gun control reduces crime will usually lead to support of gun control legislation. On the other hand, belief that the exercise of Second Amendment rights reduces crime will lead to quite a different set of behaviors, such as support of stricter enforcement of current gun laws or membership in the National Rifle Association.

Values

A *value* is an indicator of the relative worth, usefulness, or general importance of something. What a person values also has a great impact on behavior. Jim's father valued education above nearly all else. As a result, he paid for Jim's education in full, while insisting that his son perform to the best of his academic ability. By contrast, Jim's roommate, Karl came from a family that placed a high value on independence and earning your own way. As a result, Karl held several part-time jobs in order to pay his college tuition. The two student's familial values are different, and as a result, so too were their actions and activities.

Behaviors

Attitudes, beliefs, and values are mental and thus not directly observable. But *behavior* refers to observable actions. Behavior is the effect that is caused by a person's attitudes, beliefs, and values. Behavior is so important in the study of persuasion because it is a tangible measure of the change in attitudes, beliefs, and values. Behavior change is the way a speaker knows if his or her speech has had the desired impact.

- If a speaker can convince an audience member to change his/her attitude about a candidate, the speaker can change his/her behavior by winning that audience member's vote.
- If a speaker can persuade an audience member to believe that gambling is evil, that audience member's behavior will follow when he or she stops spending money on lottery tickets.
- If a speaker can argue effectively the value of daily devotions, then the audience member will alter behavior and begin to set aside a regular time for scripture reading and prayer.

Principles of Persuasion

The persuasive speaker who endeavors to change the attitudes, beliefs, values, and thus the behaviors of the audience will need to be aware of several truths about the nature of human beings and their relative openness to change. These truths are presented below as three principles of persuasion.

Principle of Variation

It is important for the persuasive public speaker to recognize that attitudes, beliefs, and values vary in strength and importance. Those attitudes, beliefs, and values that are most central to a person's being are sometimes called *core values*. The instructor of an Introduction to Theology class challenged Evan and his classmates with an unusual assignment. "I want you to make a list," he said, "of the things you would be willing to die for." Evan later remarked, "If you take an assignment like that seriously, you spend a lot of time on a very short list." Certainly whatever appears on such a list would be considered among a person's core values.

Basic values are those that are held not as strongly as core values but are still very important to a person. Denominational affiliation or theological positions are basic values for many Christians. Similarly, those who have carefully considered the opposing viewpoints may see political party affiliation as basic. And while many people purchase a vehicle on the basis of color or price, Dan saw his preference for one make over another as a basic value. "I would rather walk than drive that junk," he said firmly when speaking of a competitor's make of vehicle.

Finally, peripheral attitudes, beliefs, and values are the least important to a person. These are sometimes referred to as preferences. Matters such as what color shirt to wear, what food to eat, or where to spend spring break are all usually *peripheral values*. Certainly, most people would not be willing to die for these choices, nor are they even well thought out and thus basic to an individual's makeup.

Realizing that attitudes, beliefs, and values vary in strength and importance, the effective public speaker will set the persuasive agenda accordingly. This is accomplished on the basis of audience analysis. When Stan did a class survey prior to his speech to persuade, he discovered that 80 percent of his audience believed that the college library should be open on Sunday. No one in that target group, however, was intending to transfer to another school, picket the library, or petition administration over the hours of the library. Stan concluded that the matter was a peripheral issue for the audience. Stan, therefore, determined that in his speech he might be able to convince the audience that a day off for students and library staff was a good idea.

Principle of Consistency

Researchers agree that human beings desire *cognitive consistency*.[3] That means that individuals avoid holding two attitudes, beliefs, or values that are in opposition to one another. The state of inconsistency that comes from holding these opposing views is called *cognitive dissonance*. Such dissonance becomes a powerful motivator as individuals move to restore cognitive balance.

> *Cognitive consistency*: Individuals avoid holding two attitudes, beliefs, or values that are in opposition to one another.
>
> *Cognitive dissonance*: The effect of holding two attitudes, beliefs, or values that oppose one another.

Shawn had shopped carefully in order to made a good choice with regard to the purchase of his very first car. He had used his high school graduation gifts for the down payment on the vehicle, and had signed a note for two years of additional payments. That meant that Shawn would have to take a part-time job during his freshman year of college. On the one hand Shawn was delighted with his purchase, but on the other, it meant a job which would cut into his study time. Shawn had cognitive

---

3. See for example: Heider, *Psychology of Interpersonal Relations*; Newcomb, *The Acquaintance Process*; Osgood and Tannenbaum, "Principle of Congruity in Prediction of Attitude Change;" Festinger, *A Theory of Cognitive Dissonance*, Rokeach, *The Nature of Human Values*

dissonance about the purchase. He held two opposing views at the same time.

Sometimes when a speaker attempts to persuade an audience, the adoption of the speaker's premise will yield cognitive dissonance in audience members. Such a situation is always a very difficult persuasive task. Evelyn felt strongly that abortion was wrong. Her audience analysis revealed that most of the students in her class agreed. When Evelyn attempted to convince the audience to join her in protesting at an area abortion clinic, however, she met with a great deal of audience resistance. Her proposal to picket the clinic, draw a crowd, and probably get arrested created cognitive dissonance even in her pro-life audience. Evelyn was less successful in her persuasive speech because she failed to consider that human beings desire cognitive consistency.

Principle of Needs

A third principle, the knowledge of which helps the persuader, is that people are persuaded according to their needs. According to this principle, every individual has needs, which become that person's chief motivators.

One of the key proponents of needs theory was Abraham Maslow.[4] Maslow believed that people were persuaded according to their needs. He summarized needs in five groupings and maintained that the lower level needs had to be met before the upper level needs had motivating impact.

The lowest level needs Maslow termed *physiological needs*. These needs must be met very quickly as a matter of survival. The need for air and water are primary in this grouping.

Once physiological needs have been satisfied the *safety needs* begin to motivate an individual. Safety needs include the need for food and shelter.

Third level needs are called *love needs*. According to Maslow every human being has the need to love and to be loved. These needs begin to motivate once the lower level needs of safety and physiology have been met.

The fourth level needs are labeled *esteem needs*. Humans whose lower level needs are met are susceptible to persuasion on the basis of their need to feel good about themselves.

Finally, the highest level need is the need for *self-actualization*. Self-actualization is the need to be the best that one can be and to make a lasting difference.

---

4. Maslow, "A Theory of Human Motivation," 370–96.

> *Physiological needs*: Lowest of the five levels of needs according to Maslow's hierarchy, including the need for air and water.
>
> *Safety needs*: According to Maslow's hierarchy, the second level of needs, including the need for food and shelter.
>
> *Love needs*: Third level of needs according to Maslow's hierarchy indicating that everyone has the need to love and to be loved.
>
> *Esteem needs*: Need to feel good about self. Fourth level of needs according to Maslow's hierarchy.
>
> *Self-actualization needs*: Need to be the best one can be and to make a lasting difference, constituting the highest level on Maslow's hierarchy of needs.

The persuasive speaker will need to set the persuasive agenda according to the needs of the audience. Juan had developed an expository lesson on the power of Jesus to transform believers outreach efforts in order to make them more effective. He titled the lesson, "Be All You Can Be in God's Army" after a U.S. Army recruitment advertising campaign. The lesson was very well received at Juan's upper middle class church. When he was invited to speak at the inner city rescue mission he used the same speech. This time he got a much less favorable response. The director of the mission explained, "These men aren't into being all they can be. They are first interested in having their stomachs full and being warm for the night." With those words he offered Juan a post-address audience analysis. His counsel could well be phrased, "People are persuaded according to their needs."

Persuasive Propositions

Having considered these important principles of persuasion and determined an appropriate persuasive strategy, the persuasive speaker must now turn to the three types of statements used in a persuasive speech in order to change attitudes, beliefs, values, and thus behaviors. Statements of fact, value, and policy represent the building blocks of a persuasive speech. Understanding the three as well as the distinctions between them, serves to make the persuasive speech clearer and the persuasive appeal more compelling.

Statements of Fact

Statements of fact concern what is or is not true. These statements can be verified and are nearly universally held. The use of statements of fact helps the persuasive speaker prove or disprove a thesis.

Kim wanted to persuade her audience to become organ donors. She began with the statement of fact that organ donation saves lives. From that statement of fact her persuasive appeal was developed.

Roger wished to persuade his audience that television violence leads to violent behavior in viewers. His task became easier once he had established the fact that advertisers believe television viewing changes behavior in favor of their product. That statement of fact made it much easier for Roger to declare that since we know that television changes behavior, it is possible that it also changes toward more violent behavior.

Statements of Value

Statements of value offer moral judgments. Such statements affirm something as good or bad, moral or immoral, right or wrong. Statements of value may be only matters of personal opinion, or they may be based upon scriptural truth or some other authority. Statements of value are sometimes strengthened by the support of expert testimony or by parallel statements of fact.

In his speech to persuade, Juan intended to convince the audience to boycott professional baseball. He began with this statement of fact. "Professional baseball players are paid very large salaries, which originate from gate receipts." He buttressed the appeal with a statement of value. "Such huge salaries are unjustified and immoral."

In a similar manner, Charity wished to persuade her audience to vote for a particular mayoral candidate in her city. She too began with a statement of fact. "Candidate Young favors school vouchers as a means of education reform." She then led into a statement of value as a part of her persuasive agenda. That statement was "Choice is invaluable in developing the very best in the free enterprise system."

Statements of Policy

Statements or propositions of policy argue that a certain course of action should or should not be taken. The words *should* or *ought* usually appear or are implied in a *statement of policy*. Statements of policy which have supported student speeches to persuade include:

- Division 1 college athletes should be paid for their work.
- Christians ought to pray daily.
- The university drug policy must be enforced.
- To enhance national security, America's borders should be sealed.
- Students should not be required to perform community service.
- The general education curriculum must be altered.
- Women should not date a man who refuses to hold a door for them.
- Protestant denominations should reconcile their differences.
- As a matter of health, college students should not drink products with caffeine.

Persuasive Speech Structures

As with other types of speeches, the correct structure of a speech to persuade is a crucial element of public speaking effectiveness. One of three primary persuasive structures is usually used. These are *problem/solution*, *comparative advantages*, and *Monroe's Motivated Sequence*.

Problem/Solution

The *problem/solution* organizational structure uses two main points in order to accomplish the persuasive task. In the first main point, the speaker demonstrates that a problem exists. In the second main point of the speech, the speaker declares the preferred plan for solving the problem and supports that plan over others.

Kerry did her speech to persuade on why college students should develop an exercise program. She used the problem/solution organizational structure. In the problem section of the speech, she pointed out that college students are developing life patterns today. She also noted that good health later in life demanded more exercise. In the second section of the speech, she proposed that fitness clubs provided the most logical way to stay fit. As a part of the call to action, she provided the enrollment data for several fitness clubs in the area around her university.

As a naturalized citizen Ming enjoyed tremendous credibility on the topic of English as an official language of the United States. Ming used a problem-solution structure with the following points:

1. Legislation before Congress would make English the official language of the United States.
2. Such legislation is appropriate and important.

    a. It provides a goal for immigrants as they become a part of the nation.
    b. It preserves national unity.

Comparative Advantages

The comparative advantages structure for a speech to persuade assumes the audience's agreement on the existence of a problem. The speech focuses instead on why the proposed action of a speaker is preferable to other possible solutions. The several main parts of the speech each explain why the proposed solution is the best.

Connie sought to persuade her audience to become regular in attendance at Sunday morning worship. Each point of the speech presented a comparative advantage of attending, over not attending. Her outline looked like this:

1. Church attendance honors God.
2. Church attendance encourages self-discipline.
3. Church attendance builds friendships.
4. Church attendance fosters emotional tranquility.

Ironically, in the same speech class Jessica used comparative advantage to promote her position that the Christian university that she and Connie attended should not leave required church attendance in the student life handbook. She believed that church attendance was a personal matter that should be left to individual student. Jessica's points were

1. Required attendance is legalistic.
2. Required attendance minimizes the joy of voluntary participation.
3. Required attendance assumes student immaturity.

Monroe's Motivated Sequence

Alan Monroe developed the third persuasive speech structure, which is known as *Monroe's Motivated Sequence*.[5] His work, originally published in the 1930s, provides a clear pattern for moving an audience from the definition of a problem to a proposed solution and on to an analysis of the benefits of implementing that solution. The motivated sequence is a very popular structure for developing persuasive speeches because it carefully follows the normal process of human reasoning and thought. Monroe's

---

5. Gronbeck et al., *Principles and Types of Speech Communication*, 266–70.

Speeches to Persuade

Motivated Sequence is a five-step approach to persuasive thinking. The speaker follows these steps:

1. Attention: Here the speaker gains the audience's attention about the topic in question.
2. Need: In this step the speaker outlines the problem or need.
3. Satisfaction: The speaker proposes a solution that will meet the need.
4. Visualization: Here how the speaker's proposed solution will work and why it is preferable to other possible solutions is analyzed.
5. Action: The speaker challenges the audience to a specific course of action in order to implement the proposed solution.

Jerry used Monroe's Motivated Sequence in his speech to persuade. He had become involved in volunteer work at a nursing home a few blocks from campus and wanted to persuade others to volunteer their time as well. The five-step approach supported his proposal very well.

1. Attention: Jerry told the story of an elderly man who had no family members living in the State so he received few visits.
2. Need: Jerry presented data from the local nursing home indicating that his elderly friend was not unique. In fact, a large percentage of residents were lonely and would appreciate a visit from younger people.
3. Satisfaction: Jerry proposed that every class member volunteer just one hour per week at the home.
4. Visualization: Jerry made several points to help the audience visualize the results of such a volunteer program. These included:
   a. A combined total of twenty-five hours per week with those in need could be provided by the class as a whole.
   b. Personal joy comes from sharing with another.
   c. Joy is passed on to the residents of the nursing home through the knowledge that someone cares.

In addition, Jerry recognized in this step that two potential objections existed. He refuted each by providing solutions.

   a. "I don't have time."
   b. "I don't know what to say."

5. Action: Jerry's call to action was clear and compelling. He distributed a sign-up sheet for the current week and agreed to meet each volunteer at the nursing home to make appropriate introductions.

Persuasive Appeals

Jerry's speech appealed to the emotions of his audience. He described in detail the loneliness of his aged friend and declared that the audience members themselves had the power to change the man's lonely existence. Jerry knew that often an emotional appeal is effective in a persuasive speech. Sometimes, however, it is not the right approach. That is why Aristotle identified emotional appeal and two other forms of persuasive appeal. These appeals, or forms of proof, are commonly referred to by the Greek names which Aristotle assigned them.

Pathos

Pathos, or emotional appeal, taps into the audience's feelings in order to gain their approval for the speaker's point of view. Gwynn wanted to persuade the class audience to sponsor a child in the third world with food and school supplies. Her pictures of children in poverty held the audience's attention and accomplished her persuasive purpose.

Similarly, Porter used primarily an emotional appeal in his speech to persuade. His grandfather had been brutally murdered many years earlier. The convicted killer languished on death row. Porter used pathos to call for swifter justice in the court system.

Ethos

The second form of persuasive appeal is *ethos* or credibility. A credible speaker is a more persuasive speaker, since credibility refers to a speaker's believability. Speakers gain credibility in several important ways.

First, credibility may come from the expertise that a speaker brings on a specific topic. This type of credibility is sometimes referred to as *extrinsic credibility*, meaning that it originates outside the speech. Belsa, the roundtable participant from Honduras, will not have to mention how he knows about Honduras in his speech. He will enjoy enormous extrinsic credibility without saying a word.

> *Extrinsic credibility*: Credibility that a speaker brings to the speech and that originates outside the speaking event. Contrast *intrinsic credibility*.

Sometimes credibility comes from within the speech itself. This is referred to as *intrinsic credibility*. Speaking with conviction and authority, revealing personal experiences, and using technical terms appropriately all lead to intrinsic credibility. Sarah gained intrinsic credibility for her speech to persuade on universal health care when she began her speech by saying, "Being brought up in a home with two medical professionals for parents has given me a unique perspective on the issues surrounding universal health care."

> *Intrinsic credibility*: Credibility that comes from within the speech itself as a result of the speaker's charisma or expertise. Contrast *extrinsic credibility*.

Logos

The Greek word *logos* literally means "word" and is the third of Aristotle's persuasive appeals. It is used to refer to the logical appeals that a speaker uses to persuade an audience. A speaker uses logos when appealing on the basis of the form or substance of an argument.

Ethan offered a brilliant persuasive speech on universal health care. He debunked many of the emotionally based myths surrounding the topic and gave a strong presentation of facts. He pointed out logically that universal care would not be free health care. The issue, he noted, involves who will pay the health care bills in America. Ethan's appeals were formulated primarily from logos.

The Chapter in Brief

Persuasion is the process by which a speaker elicits a voluntary change in the attitudes, beliefs, values, and thus behaviors of another. These four: attitudes, beliefs, values, and behavior are the elements of persuasion.

Three principles of persuasion are noted by the most persuasive public speakers. These include:

- Principle of Variation
- Principle of Consistency
- Principle of Needs

Upon these principles the successful persuader builds his or her case with:

- Statements of Fact
- Statements of Value

- Statements of Policy

Often when constructing a speech to persuade the speaker will use one of three primary organizational structures. These are:
- Problem/Solution
- Comparative Advantages
- Monroe's Motivated Sequence

Finally, some speeches to persuade will use primarily persuasive appeals of emotion, or pathos. Others will rely more heavily on appeals to credibility, or ethos. The third type of persuasive appeal is the appeal to logic, or logos. In reality some combination of the three persuasive appeals is most likely to yield success.

Key Terms

Use the list below to test your knowledge of the vocabulary introduced in this chapter.

- reversal strategy
- reinforcement strategy
- persuasion
- attitude
- belief
- values
- behavior
- statement of fact
- statement of value
- statement of policy
- cognitive consistency
- cognitive dissonance
- core values
- basic values
- peripheral values
- physiological needs
- safety needs
- love needs
- esteem needs
- self-actualization needs
- extrinsic credibility
- problem/solution structure
- comparative advantage

- Monroe's motivated sequence
- ethos
- pathos
- logos
- intrinsic credibility

For Review and Discussion

1. Ryan argued at the roundtable discussion that it was impossible for a speaker to persuade on a topic where there is already agreement. Do you agree or disagree? Explain your answer.
2. List some of your own core values. Compare your list to others in your class or discussion group.
3. We know that audience members desire cognitive consistency. What impact does that information have on the importance of audience analysis?

Proclamation Practice

Select one of the topics below and prepare a five to seven minute speech to persuade. Use Monroe's Motivated Sequence.

- Gun control
- Universal health care
- Human cloning
- School vouchers
- "Right to die" legislation
- Same-sex marriage
- City-wide smoking bans
- Homosexuals in the church

11

Speeches to Edify

Chapter Challenges

A careful reading of Chapter 11 will provide insights into these chapter challenges:

1. What is a speech to edify?
2. What are the three primary types of speeches to edify?
3. What five components usually appear in a testimony speech?

4. What is an expository lesson?
5. What is a faith lesson?
6. How does a faith lesson differ from an expository lesson? How are they the same?

At the Student Union Roundtable

"I hate busy work," said Cynthia as she took her seat at the student union roundtable. "And busy work is all there is to this testimony speech that we are all working on."

"How do you figure it is busy work?" quizzed Jess.

"Yeah, I'm curious too. I thought the assignment had a very practical side," agreed Janelle.

"I don't think I'd go so far as to call it practical," said Belsa in an attempt to mediate. "But neither did I see it as busy work. Dr. Connelly said the thesis statement is to be 'In this speech I will introduce myself to my audience by describing my personal faith walk.'"

"Right," continued Cynthia. "That is a testimony and at this college everyone is already a Christian. In fact, they have to write out a testimony on their application to even be considered for admission. So giving a testimony speech here is just busy work."

"I think I see the problem now," Ryan inserted. "You're suggesting that the only reason to give a testimony is to win people to Christ. Since your audience analysis concludes that your audience is made up of those who already believe, the speech has no practical value."

"Bingo," said Cynthia. "At least someone gets my point. Like I said, it is nothing but busy work."

Edification

Cynthia has made the mistake of assuming that evangelism is the only reason to develop a testimony speech. That assumption would put the assignment into the speech to persuade category, and if her audience analysis correctly concludes that everyone in the audience is a believer, it may be that Cynthia is correct in assuming the speech has little practical value. Certainly, given the assumptions, the speech has little opportunity to accomplish its' intended purpose.

Successful evangelism, winning persons to Christ,[1] is only one purpose of a speech that describes an individual's faith walk. A testimony

---

1. Murphree, *Responsible Evangelism*, 13.

speech for those who already comprise the body of Christ takes on a much different general purpose. With those who are already a part of the church as the audience, a testimony speech becomes a speech to edify.

The term *edification* means to instruct or improve the mind by means of moral or spiritual teaching. Speeches that edify offer spiritual truths in order to encourage, improve, or build up the minds of the audience with regard to Christian teaching and the Christian life. These speeches are closely associated with what some refer to as "speeches of inspiration."[2] Speeches to edify generally fit into one of three types including *testimony speeches*, *expository lessons*, and *faith lessons*.

Christian Testimonies

A *Christian testimony* is a speech that indicates how a believer came to faith in Jesus Christ, or how he or she has grown in that faith. It is a Christian's statement of a personal faith walk. As with the use of general testimony as a supporting data, such a statement is extremely powerful. It may be reinterpreted by an audience, but its statement of fact can rarely be successfully challenged. It is the speaker's personal experience.

The Apostle Paul used personal testimony in his edification speeches.[3] So have countless other Christians down through the ages. The statement of Christian experience seems to be one of the ways that the Lord has ordained to spread the truth of his kingdom.

Sometimes a testimony has a specialized theme, such as "What I Learned Recently about the Great Commission" or "A Lifetime of Prayer." Other times the testimony is a general statement. The latter often follows a five-step outline.

Introduction

In the opening sentences of a testimony speech, a speaker will need to establish rapport with the audience. This is accomplished by means of an introduction. The introduction step has very similar features to those already discussed for a speech to inform or a speech to persuade. That is, the speaker will need to:

- Capture the attention of the audience
- Build rapport with the audience
- Motivate the audience to listen
- Preview the speech for the audience

2. O'Hair, et al., *Speaker's Guidebook*, 403.
3. Barnette, "I Stand Here Testifying," 22–26.

Since the general testimony speech is a life story, the speaker is often tempted to choose a chronological ordering for the speech. That temptation is usually best avoided. Instead successful speakers select a life-theme or a recurring lesson to capture the attention of the audience and become the main focus of the speech.

When Mike gave his testimony speech, he wanted to emphasize a turning point in his life that came while he was on a mission's trip to Honduras. But at first, Mike used a chronological ordering for the speech. His introduction began, "I was born in a small town just outside of Chicago. Since both of my parents were Christians, I was raised in the church and considered myself a disciple at an early age. But on a mission's trip to Honduras, something happened to challenge all of my assumptions and transform my life."

Mike's instructor previewed the introduction and told Mike she believed it was adequate but not exceptional. She suggested that Mike put aside his commitment to chronological ordering and try again. Mike's second attempt focused on what make him a unique individual. It emphasized what set Mike apart from his peers. And not surprisingly, it accomplished all of the elements of a great introduction. The new introduction said,

"I could not understand a word that anyone spoke."

"The high-mountain terrain was unlike anything I had ever experienced before."

"Everyone looked different from me."

"The food was definitely not from Illinois."

"In short, even in a crowded Latin American city, I had never felt so lonely in all of my life. And God chose that moment, when I was farthest from my comfort zone, to speak to me with a life-changing message. Today I want to share with you what I learned about myself while in Tegucigalpa, Honduras, and how that lesson changed my life."

Before Christ

In order to demonstrate the change that Christ brings into a life in the clearest possible way, it is often necessary to provide a word picture of life before conversion. The length and impact of this portion of the speech will vary with each individual speaker.

Dave grew up in a Christian home. He jokingly noted, "I've attended the same church since nine months before I was born." While Dave believed in the importance of making a personal decision for Jesus Christ, he necessarily had only a brief before Christ statement to offer.

Sometimes speakers mistakenly assume that a short before Christ statement means the speaker actually has no testimony. Nowhere in scripture, however, does it indicate that in order to be a solid disciple one must have experienced the horrors of a life of sin. One student summed it up when she noted, "In Acts 16 it says that all members of the household of the Philippian jailor were baptized that same night. Surely the little children among them were not later considered less than full disciples, provided they had confirmed their father's earlier decision as their own."

On the other hand, some speakers find the before Christ portion of their speech to be a major segment. Angie realized during the campus fall revival during her freshman year at a Christian university that her life did not model Christian values. Her parents were Christians and had insisted that she attend their alma mater. But Angie had never really adopted her parents' faith as her own. On Wednesday in chapel she went forward and committed to Christ. The following Tuesday she gave her testimony speech in public speaking class. Angie's before Christ section of the speech proved to be the most lengthy.

Those who do have longer before Christ sections must take special care to properly articulate the nature of a life without Christ. Honesty is a must, but sin should not be glorified or described in inappropriate detail. Every aspect of the speech must always be appropriate for the entire audience. This appropriateness is determined through careful audience analysis.[4] The purpose of the speech is to edify by holding up Christ, not to focus on a life of sin.

Conversion

Various theological understandings and ecclesiastical groups hold to different views on the nature of conversion. The speaker will need to exercise care therefore, to see that the speech does not provide undo offense to listeners. The best rule of thumb is to provide as many details and as clear an understanding as can be done with integrity.

JoLynn offered a one-statement conversion in her testimony speech. She said, "I honestly cannot remember a time before Jesus was the clear focus and central theme of my life." Many of her classmates had first-hand experience with her situation.

Lacy on the other hand, provided the date, time, place, and even a detailed statement as to the feelings that accompanied her decision to

---

4. Ibid.

follow Christ. Her audience responded with similar understanding and appreciation.

The effective speaker always provides as many details as possible. That is because the speaker's credibility hinges upon the ability to state such details with believable accuracy.

During the conversion section of his testimony speech Roy stated, "I don't really remember any conversion experience. I guess I was just born a Christian." Roy's classmates raised both theological and credibility questions on their peer reviews. Since Roy's experience did not match that of most of the audience members, Roy needed to more carefully articulate what he meant by being born a Christian.

Susan's conversion statement was better, but it also lacked sufficient detail. She said, "Sometime during my high school career I became a serious Christian." Such a general statement left the audience wondering about the validity of Susan's experience and the genuineness of the change she described. "Certainly such a life change would carry with it accompanying details," they reasoned.

Connie actually had no more recollection than Susan of the precise day and time of her belief. But Connie enjoyed enormous credibility when she said, "It honestly was not significant enough at the time for me to note the date, but the committal service at youth camp the summer after my sophomore year, I now know was a moment that changed my life for time and eternity." Adding appropriate details made Connie's statement very effective.

Since Christ

One of the most often neglected aspects of a speech of personal testimony involves what has happened since the speaker came to a saving knowledge of Christ. This was evident at a Sunday evening service in a small local church where an elderly gentleman gave his "testimony." He said, "Well, preacher, it was 1947 and I had just returned from the big war. We had a revival in this church with Reverend E. Z. Hunt as evangelist. On the first evening, September 17 at about 8:45, Reverend Hunt gave the invitation. I knelt down right there at that altar, about four feet to the left of where you are standing right now, and met Jesus. And my life has never been the same. Amen."

With that the man sat down leaving the pastor and the rest of his audience to wonder, "Has Jesus done anything in your life since 1947?"

Good speakers avoid missing the "since Christ" step in their testimony speech. During the preparation process the speaker will want to ask several self-examination questions. Among them:

- What is the focus of my spiritual growth right now?
- What is the cutting edge for me spiritually?
- How has my spiritual life changed in the last six months?
- Why did I choose my particular university? Or major? Or spouse?
- What was God's role in that decision?
- How do I currently view God's plan for my life?

These questions and others like them will help the speaker develop the since Christ section.

The time allotted for the since Christ portion of a testimony speech is usually inversely proportional to the before Christ section. That is, the place where a speaker has spent the most time should also occupy most of the speech. New converts will offer an abbreviated section of since Christ activities, while those who have years of experience as a disciple will reflect that more extensive experience.

Challenge

As Cynthia noted at the round table discussion, sometimes the purpose of a testimony is evangelism through persuasion. The final portion of the speech in that case will be a clear call to Christian discipleship. On the other hand, the speech to edify is designed to enlighten and build up those who are already disciples. In this case the final challenge of the speech will be different.

For example, when Terri gave her testimony speech before her public speaking class she wanted to convince them that all Christians should pray for non-Christians just as her aunt had prayed for her. Terri's very effective challenge involved asking each member of the audience to select one person for whom they would commit to regular prayer.

The challenge of a testimony speech should serve a similar purpose to the conclusion of a speech to inform or a speech to persuade. The challenge should:

- Summarize the key points of the speech
- Make those points memorable
- Encourage audience members to actively engage in Christian discipleship

The Christian testimony is an important speech to edify. Properly prepared and delivered this type of speech builds up the body of Christ for service. So too does a second type of speech to edify, the *expository lesson*.

Expository Lessons

The word *expository* is derived from the Latin, "expositio," which means to set forth the meaning or expound upon. Expository lessons are those which set forth the meaning or expound upon a truth from the biblical text.

Many pastors use expository preaching, which is preaching designed to expose and expound upon the truth of a particular biblical passage. In fact, some suggest that any sermon other than expository is not truly biblical preaching.[5] While it is debatable whether or not all sermons must be expository, it is clear that not all expository lessons must be sermons. Sunday school lessons and class devotions are but two additional examples of this type of speech to edify.

The expository lesson is unique, not because of the audience or the setting, but because of the relationship of the speech to a biblical text. Robinson summarizes the relationship of the sermon or speech to a biblical passage. He recognizes this type of message as one which:

- Gets the idea from the passage
- Honors the development of the passage
- Reflects the purpose of the passage
- Grapples with the truth of the passage[6]

Clearly the public speaker engaged in the preparation of an expository lesson must first accomplish an accurate interpretation of the biblical text.[7]

Exegesis

The purpose of expository communication is to relate the essential truth of a text by means of the scripture itself.[8] The speaker must somehow discover that essential truth. The systematic study designed to discover the original intended meaning of a scripture passage is called *exegesis*.

Exegesis is best accomplished when the speaker approaches the Scripture as a detective might view a crime scene.[9] In the exegetical process,

---

5. Stott, Between Two Worlds, 126.
6. Robinson, "The Relevance of Expository Preaching," 79–93.
7. McDill, The Moment of Truth, 17–19.
8. Olford, Anointed Expository Preaching, 69–76.
9. Traina, *Methodical Bible Study*, 3.

the speaker looks for the facts revealed by the text itself. Traina suggests a four-step approach to this "methodical Bible study." The four steps include:

- Observation
- Interpretation
- Evaluation
- Correlation[10]

Carefully following the step by step approach encourages the speaker to let the biblical text speak and offer its clear meaning.

Observation occurs when the speaker examines the biblical text without partiality. The question "What does the passage actually say?" guides the study. The speaker consciously leaves behind personal preconceptions, as well as those of others who have previously engaged in an exegesis of the passage.

> *Observation*: First step in methodical Bible study, involving asking, without preconceptions, what the passage is saying.

Interpretation raises the question "What does it mean?" This step encourages the speaker to recreate the historic context of the biblical text. The process seeks to discover the intended purpose of the passage or text.

> *Interpretation:* Second step of methodical Bible study that raises the question "What does the passage mean?"

Evaluation, sometimes referred to as "application," seeks to discover the value of the passage for the modern reader. Sometimes the word *hermeneutics* is applied to the search for this contemporary relevance of ancient truths.[11] In the previous two steps, the speaker has withheld value judgments about the passage. Now that the observation and interpretation steps are complete, the speaker is searching for the timeless truth in the passage.

---

10. Ibid., 31, 91, 203, 223.
11. Fee and Stuart, *How To Read The Bible for All It's Worth*, 29.

> *Evaluation*: Third step in methodical Bible study, involving a search for the timeless truths in the passage. Also called "application."

Finally, the speaker engages in *correlation*. In this step the timeless truths discovered during the evaluation process are blended with those timeless truths previously discovered. The end result, over time, for the careful and consistent expository speaker, is the development of a comprehensive biblical theology. In a single expository lesson, the speaker must take great care to practice consistency with the whole of the biblical text.

> *Correlation*: The final step in methodical Bible study that involves blending the truths of a passage with timeless truths previously discovered.

The beginning speaker who develops an expository lesson may lack confidence in his or her personal ability to properly interpret the text. As a result, many a speaker has yielded to the temptation to begin with a commentary. At first glance, it seems prudent to seek the word of another professional interpreter. But the careful biblical study necessary for developing the expository lesson should always begin with direct observation and personal interpretation. Referral to an outside source may later be used to confirm the study or when the speaker is stuck for additional observations. The process of exegesis is designed to first and foremost let the text speak for itself.

Outlining

Sometimes the biblical passage will provide even the outline of the speech. When Brittany developed a Sunday school lesson on the stages of the Christian life, her outline came directly from Acts 16:23–34. Brittany declared in her introduction that the Philippian jailer who is introduced in that passage, had gone through four stages of spiritual development in one night. The stages Brittany spoke on were:

1. Sinner (verses 23–24)
2. Seeker (verse 30)
3. Son (verses 31–32)
4. Servant (verses 33–34)

Speeches to Edify

For Donald's class devotion he used an expository lesson. The biblical text that he used was accurately and clearly developed. Donald's outline did not, however, come directly from the text. He used as a springboard Paul's words, "By the grace of God, I am what I am." Donald discussed several types of grace that Paul may have had in mind when he said, "By the grace of God, I am what I am." His main points included:

1. Saving Grace
2. Cleansing Grace
3. Healing Grace
4. Protecting Grace

Donald's speech was clearly expository. It accurately reflected not only Paul's words at this one point but a great deal of his entire life. The outline however came from several passages of scripture instead of just the one in question.

Sometimes the speaker will need to develop a speech where not only the outline, but several key points as well, do not directly appear in the pages of scripture. Then the more appropriate speech to edify is the *faith lesson*.

Faith Lessons

Faith lessons are those speeches to edify that do not come directly from the study of a particular scripture passage, but do support the clear general teachings of the Bible and the Christian faith. Since the church views scripture as the authoritative word of the living God, the speaker who wishes to communicate truth will always begin with the source of all truth, the scripture.[12]

However, the Bible does not address every situation about which a speaker may need to communicate in order to provide edification for the audience.[13] Points of theology, doctrinal lessons, some matters related to the Christian life, and certain modern social issues for example may not be directly addressed in the pages of scripture. The speaker will need to approach these topics with the faith lesson.

For example, Christina wanted to address what it means for humans to be created in the image of God in her speech to edify. She carefully examined Genesis, Chapter two in a futile attempt to develop an expository lesson. Finally she used several theology books as sources and put together

---

12. Gibson, "Biblical Preaching in an Anti-authority Age," 215–27.
13. Allen, Preaching: *An Essential Guide*, 40–41.

a faith lesson on the topic. Her outline stressed the ways that humans are created in God's image.

1. The natural image of God
   a. Spirituality
   b. Immortality
2. The moral image of God
   a. Capacity to provide a temple for the Holy Spirit
   b. Capacity for holy living

Clearly, Christina's faith lesson was biblically accurate. It was also topical in its organization.

Frank addressed the issues relating to world hunger in his speech to edify. He developed a faith lesson rather than an expository lesson. Frank used the acronym "care" for the outline of his speech. His four suggestions on how to address the problems of world hunger were:

1. Combine local with worldwide responses
2. Ask God for direction
3. Reduce personal consumption
4. Enlist the help of others

In addressing the development of faith lessons, Allen, who refers to such lessons as "topical," offers a series of five preparation steps.[14] These include, first, carefully defining the topic. The fact that a speaker is not limited by the scope of a particular biblical passage does not excuse rambling on tangential matters.

Second, the speaker must carefully relate the topic to the needs of the audience today. Faith lessons should clearly have modern, practical, and relevant application.

Third, the speaker should seek to discover the history of the topic. What are the origins of the topic? How have others both historically and in contemporary thought viewed the topic?

Fourth, how does the church view the topic? Often a faith lesson will expose the contrast between the attitudes on a particular topic of those who hold to a Christian worldview with those whose outlook is secular.

Fifth, how do different Christians perceive the topic? Whereas in expository lessons the word of truth must not be compromised on the basis of divergent beliefs, in a faith lesson there may well be equally valid points of view within a Christian worldview.

14 Ibid., 42–48.

Finally, to Allen's steps the careful Christian speaker will add the question, "What does the Bible say on the topic?" The speaker has a moral and ethical responsibility to see that even though faith lessons do not spring directly from the Bible, they never contradict the Bible. This guarantee of biblical accuracy makes the development of effective faith lessons at least as difficult and time consuming as their expository counterparts.

The Chapter in Brief

Speeches to edify seek to instruct or improve the minds of those who are a part of the Christian community. They generally fall into one of three types:

- Testimony speeches
- Expository lessons
- Faith lessons

Testimony speeches relate an individual's personal faith walk. They are usually developed around a five-part structure. The steps of a testimony speech include:

- Introduction
- Before Christ
- Conversion
- Since Christ
- Challenge

Expository lessons are speeches that set forth or expand upon the meaning of a Biblical text. Such speeches involve a careful and thorough practice of Bible study.

Faith lessons are speeches that address topics not specifically covered in a particular biblical passage, but which never the less are vital to the Christian community. Faith lessons are biblically accurate but generated from sources other than the exposition of the biblical text.

Key Terms

Use the list below to test your knowledge of the vocabulary introduced in this chapter.

- edification
- observation
- Christian testimony

- interpretation
- expository lessons
- evaluation
- faith lessons
- correlation
- exegesis

For Review and Discussion

1. Some speech experts argue that speeches to edify should not be a separate category, but that every speech is either a speech to inform or a speech to persuade. Do you agree or disagree? Support your answer.

2. Report to your class or study group on the sermon you heard in church last Sunday. Compare and contrast the messages. Into which of the three categories of speeches to edify did the sermon most closely fit?

Proclamation Practice

Develop a speech to edify of six to eight minutes. Use as the topic sentence for your speech "In this speech I will build up my audience's faith by describing my own personal spiritual pilgrimage."

12

Speeches to Celebrate

Chapter Challenges

A careful reading of Chapter 12 will provide insights into these chapter challenges:

1. What is a speech to celebrate?
2. List some of the common speeches to celebrate. How are these differentiated from one another?
3. What delivery keys are especially important to the speech to celebrate?

At the Student Union Roundtable

There was a respectful silence around the student union roundtable. Ryan had just told the group of the passing of his grandfather, with whom he had been particularly close.

"You certainly have our sympathy and prayers," said Jess, breaking the silence.

"We'll all help anyway we can," agreed Cynthia.

"Thank you for your concern," Ryan said. "I appreciate your support. In fact there is something you can do to help. I have been asked to give a eulogy at the service. Help me remember some of the principles we learned in speech class in order to get started."

"First, you would need to decide what type of speech you're doing," Belsa said. "I suppose it is a speech to inform. There will be people in the audience who didn't know your grandfather as well as you did. You'll want to inform them about his life."

"I thought it would be a speech to persuade," Janelle objected. "Won't Ryan's task be to persuade the rest of the people at the memorial service to view his grandfather's life as he does?"

"Don't forget that Grandpa was a strong Christian," Ryan said. "In fact, he is the reason I'm a Christian today and the reason that I choose this Christian university. It seems like any appropriate eulogy will need to encourage people in their faith and build up the body of Christ. Are you sure it's not a speech to edify that we need?"

"I see elements of all three. Is it a speech to inform, a speech to persuade, or a speech to edify?" Jess asked. "How can we prepare an appropriate speech if we don't even know what type speech we're working on?"

Special Occasions

Jess is right. Some speeches do appear to fit into all three of the general speech types. In other situations none of the three seem appropriate. Often these scenarios call for a *speech of celebration*. Many speech professionals refer to these as *special occasion speeches*.[1] Either term is appropriate since special occasion speeches are designed to celebrate a specific event. Ryan's eulogy for example, will celebrate the life of his grandfather on the occasion of the older man's death.

---

1. O'Hair, et al., *Speaker's Guidebook: Text and Reference*, 393.

> *Speech to celebrate*: Speeches designed to celebrate a specific event or person.

Clearly, there exist a variety of special occasion needs that a speaker may be called upon to meet with a speech to celebrate. Each occasion and each type of speech will have unique characteristics. The speech to celebrate, therefore, requires a unique audience analysis.

An analysis of the event involves exploring the setting in which the speech will be delivered. It is important to establish whether the total program is monolithic or polylithic. *Monolithic programs* are composed of one principal speaker. *Polylithic programs*, on the other hand, may have several speakers at the same event. Some polylithic programs, such as conventions, may last for several days. The polished speaker at a polylithic event will search for ways to acknowledge and support the speeches of the other participants.

> *Monolithic program:* Program composed of one principal speaker.
>
> *Polylithic program:* Program composed of several speakers at the same event.

Analysis also involves the makeup of the audience itself. Some speeches to celebrate are delivered to an *ongoing assembly*. An ongoing assembly is a group such as a church group, social service organization, or club that meets regularly beyond the immediate speech context. For an ongoing assembly, the speaker may want to acknowledge the group's ministry or service and take special care to apply that work to the immediate topic.

By contrast, a *one-time assembly* has come together for a unique purpose. As a result, the one-time assembly provides a unique rhetorical event. The speaker will need to emphasize the event more than the group or its makeup. In addition, the speaker may want to challenge the various constituency groups represented by audience members to even greater service or ministry.

> *Ongoing assembly:* Group such as a church, social service organization, or club that meets regularly beyond the immediate speech context.
>
> *One-time assembly:* Group which has come together for a unique purpose, and thus creates a unique rhetorical event.

Since each special occasion is different, an appropriate speech will also be unique. There is no such thing as an effective celebration speech for every occasion. However, the speech to celebrate often fits into one of eight general occasions. These include speeches to:

- Eulogize
- Welcome
- Introduce
- Toast
- Nominate
- Accept
- Dedicate
- Entertain

Eulogy

A *eulogy* is a speech to celebrate the life of a person who has died. The word eulogy comes from the Greek prefix *good* along with the word *logos* or *word*. Hence the eulogy is literally a "good word" about someone. Eulogies are frequently a part of a funeral or memorial service for someone who has recently died.

In general eulogies accomplish three goals. They should:

1. Acknowledge the loss for both the speaker and the audience of the one being eulogized
2. Celebrate the life of the deceased
3. Encourage the mourners

It is especially important for a eulogy speaker to be honest without going overboard. Every human being has negative as well as positive qualities. While the former should not be the focus of the eulogy, neither should the speaker enhance the positives to super-human levels.[2] Honest appreciation and praise are appropriate.

Many believe that the November 6, 2002, memorial service of the late Minnesota Senator, Paul Wellstone, featured eulogies that were overzealous in their praise for the deceased. Later, Republican Norm Coleman won Wellstone's Senate seat and credited the memorial service that turned into a rally for his political victory. Apparently voters, who constituted a kind of extended audience, believed that the eulogies went beyond appropriate praise.[3]

On rare occasions speakers are called upon to eulogize someone they did not know personally. This may happen to the leader of a large organization or business who is called upon to eulogize a volunteer or employee. Clergy also sometimes must prepare a eulogy for people they did not know. In such situations the best special occasion speakers contact family members or friends in advance in order to gain as much insight as possible into the life of the one to be eulogized.[4]

The best eulogies build upon an interest or unique characteristic of the subject person. While the words of comfort and encouragement may be universally applicable, they should grow out of the subject's life. In one case the eulogy for an airplane pilot was entitled "When I Fly Away." On another occasion a long-time railroad buff was eulogized around the theme "Jesus as Engineer."

One of the most difficult aspects of the eulogy speech is delivery. That is because often the speaker knew the deceased very well and is therefore in the midst of grief in addition to the anxiety of public speaking. Some experts go so far as to declare that a speaker should refuse to deliver a eulogy if composure poses a potential problem.[5] On the other hand, audiences tend to be very understanding and sympathetic on such occasions. Also, delivery difficulties are minimized when the speaker practices delivery before the event. Some eulogists choose to use a well-rehearsed manuscript style because of the intensity of delivering this type of speech.

Welcome

A speech to welcome is a celebration speech designed to greet an individual or group. *Welcome speeches* should make people feel comfortable

   2. O'Hair, et al., *Speaker's Guidebook*, 401.
   3. Kenworthy, "Rally at Wellstone Memorial Cited in GOP Victory in Minnesota."
   4. Verderber and Verderber, *The Challenge of Effective Speaking*, 301.
   5. Sprague and Stewart, *The Speaker's Handbook*, 323.

in temporary new surroundings. Usually, the one delivering a welcome speech speaks on behalf of an organization, community, or group. It is, therefore, necessary for the speaker to be well informed about the nature of the body that he or she represents.

For example, often the mayor of a community or president of an organization gives the welcome speech in order to greet a convention or other organizational gathering. In these situations the speaker may provide some indication of the purpose of the gathering. This helps other speakers by setting the stage for what follows.

On other occasions the welcome is addressed to just one individual. Civic organizations sometimes have visitors from another chapter or club. A simple, one-paragraph welcome speech is in order on such occasions.

Sometimes a *master of ceremonies* delivers the speech of welcome. A master of ceremonies is the individual responsible for setting the general tone of a program and for keeping the event moving. As a result, the master of ceremonies may deliver celebratory comments beyond the welcome speech throughout the course of a program.

> *Master of ceremonies:* Individual responsible for setting the general tone of a program and for keeping the event moving.

Introduction

One of the most common celebration speeches is the speech of introduction. A *speech of introduction* is a speech in which the speaker introduces another for a more featured address. It might be thought of as a welcome speech for the featured speaker. Even individuals who do not perceive themselves as public speakers and would do anything to get out of standing before a crowd will eventually be called upon to deliver a speech of introduction.

That is precisely what happened when Yvonne was asked to provide devotions for the singles group at her church. Yvonne was especially introverted and had no intention of getting up in front of the group of twenty to twenty-five of her peers for a speech of edification. Thus she invited a co-worker who attended another church to prepare the devotion in her place. To her horror, when the meeting came to order, the leader said, "Yvonne, thank you for planning for our devotions this evening. Will you please introduce you friend so that we can begin?"

Unlike Yvonne's performance, the best speeches of introduction are not impromptu. Instead they are well prepared and carefully delivered speeches designed to accomplish two important goals. First, the speech of introduction provides data about the speaker. It helps the audience to feel comfortable in the presence of the previously unknown keynoter.

Second, the speech lends credibility to the speaker. In many situations requiring a speech of introduction, the audience has no previous experience with the featured speaker, but they do know the one introducing. The effective speech of introduction, therefore, declares, "You know me and trust me. Please pass that trust on to our featured speaker."

These two goals are best accomplished when the speaker preparing a speech of introduction relies on four keys to effectiveness. These keys are:

- Be brief
- Be accurate
- Be enthusiastic
- Be other-oriented

Be Brief

Appropriate brevity is essential for an effective speech of introduction. In nearly every case, audience members have come to hear the featured speaker, not the one doing the introducing. On the other hand, the speech must be long enough to provide the data an audience member needs in order to make a decision on whether or not to listen to the featured speaker.

At a fundraiser for his high school, senior class mission's trip, Justus agreed to introduce the mayor of the city. Justus realized that everyone already knew the mayor. In addition Justus felt overwhelmed by anxiety. As a result, his speech of introduction included just three words, "Here's the mayor." The event was as informal as the mayor was gracious. Justus's social blunder was quickly dismissed. But Justus did learn that effective speakers remain brief while providing enough information to interest the audience in listening.

Be Accurate

Accuracy is important in every public speaking opportunity. No where is it more important, however, than in a speech of introduction. When Terrace introduced the guest speaker for the Fellowship of Christian Athletes annual banquet, he mistakenly referred to the speaker's hometown as Beechwood, Ohio, and to his wife as Joan. When the speaker came to the lectern, he began by noting that he hailed from Oakwood, Ohio, and his wife was Jean. Since one of the goals of a speech of introduction involves lending credibility to the featured speaker, Terrace certainly failed in the assignment. In fact, his personal credibility had also been damaged as a result of the inaccuracies.

Be Enthusiastic

In order to motivate an audience to listen to a speaker, the one doing the introduction must demonstrate his or her own enthusiasm for the event. In Jeremy's introduction of a classmate to give his testimony in chapel, Jeremy began, "While most of have come to see these testimony days as just a waste of time, I think you will agree that today's speaker is about as good as it gets." Jeremy's lack of enthusiasm was contagious. The audience did not support the featured speaker as well as they might have had Jeremy provided a more enthusiastic introduction.

Introductions are a bit like the warm up act at a concert. When the introducer leaves the stage, the crowd should be ready for the main event. Enthusiastic but honest delivery style is, therefore, essential to a quality speech of introduction.

Be Other-oriented

Especially when the featured speaker is a prominent individual, the introducing speaker may be tempted to focus on his or her personal relationship with the one being introduced. One such speech began, "Tonight's speaker and I have been the best of friends for many years. We first met when . . . "

But quality speeches of introduction focus on the other, not on the self or the relationship with the other. The key is to provide enough data about the object of the introduction to whet the appetite of the audience members and lend credibility to the speaker.

Toast

A *toast* is a brief tribute in honor of an individual or group of individuals. The name for this type of speech probably comes from Roman times when a piece of burnt toast was sometimes added to cheap wine in order to absorb the unpleasant impurities in the beverage.[6] Toasts in those days were required by law as an offering to the emperor.

6. Kissell, "The Toast," 1.

Speeches to Celebrate

Centuries later in France it was customary for men to always offer a toast to any women present at a banquet. That custom evolved to our present practice of toasting the bride at a wedding.[7]

Today's toasts are usually very brief speeches to celebrate, usually lasting only one or two sentences. They are often delivered at wedding receptions or rehearsals, birthday celebrations, awards banquets, retirement parties, or business dinners. The best toasts make a single point and provide a brief example or illustration.

In addition to brevity, sincerity resulting from a personal friendship with the one being toasted is a tremendous plus for the one offering a toast. A good toast uses specific illustrations or examples that highlight a particular characteristic of the one being honored. When these examples lead to humor being used in a toast, great care must be taken to avoid embarrassing the subject or leaving the audience with questions about the "inside joke."

A toast is usually followed by raising glasses, symbolic of "drinking to" the object of the toast. The practice comes from an earlier day when it was believed that the tinkling of glasses served to ward off evil spirits.[8] Etiquette requires that the toast be offered only after everyone has been served the beverage. In modern times it is appropriate to offer a toast with either an alcoholic or non-alcoholic beverage.[9] In either case the lifted glass is a symbol of respect and honor.

Nominate

A speech to nominate places the name of an individual before a group for elected office or to receive an honor or award. Every four years the major political parties in the United States hear *speeches of nomination* as they select a candidate for president. In shorter speeches and in more local venues, candidates are similarly nominated for student government positions, or for offices within the governmental structure of the city.

Speeches of nomination have three elements that are uniquely blended. First, the speech is usually a speech to inform as the speaker outlines the requirements for the honor or office.

Second, the nominee's accomplishments are touted. The best speeches of nomination note how these accomplishments indicate the nominee's ability to fulfill the position or how the nominee deserves the honor or award.

---

7. Post, *Emily Post's Wedding Etiquette*, 366.
8. Ibid., 366.
9. Gelles-Cole, *Letitia Baldridge's Complete Guide to Executive Manners*, 352–55.

Finally, a speech of nomination should conclude with a clear appeal for support of the nominee. As a result, it might be successfully argued that the speech of nomination is in reality a speech to persuade. While it features a call to action, the first two elements do create a unique public speaking event.

Accept

A *speech to accept* is a brief statement designed to acknowledge an honor or award. Persons just nominated usually offer an acceptance speech. Such speeches are common at ceremonies like the Academy or Grammy Awards. Effective speeches of acceptance demonstrate humility as they express appreciation. The speech should express genuine thanks and acknowledge others who may have played a role in making the award or honor possible.

Entertainers seem to be divided on the question of mixing other purposes, such as politics, with acceptance speeches in a forum such as the Grammy or Academy Awards.[10] But public speaking experts agree that one should never take advantage of the occasion of an acceptance speech to launch into political statements or publicize a personal agenda. A carefully crafted thesis statement will help the acceptance speech speaker to stay focused on the real purpose at hand throughout the preparation and speaking process.

Dedicate

A *speech to dedicate* honors a person by associating their name with a permanent fixture such as a building, room, monument, or plaque. The dedication of the Clinton Presidential Library in Little Rock, Arkansas in November, 2004, provided the forum for former United States Presidents to deliver speeches of dedication. The speakers' focus on the dedication rather than their personal political differences made the event especially noteworthy.[11]

Similarly, Jill delivered a dedication speech when her church named the new church lounge after her late grandmother. Jill believed that the purpose of the speech was to convince the audience that her grandmother deserved and would have appreciated such an honor. Jill recalled her grandmother's passion for ministry at that particular church. She recalled how

---

10. Serpick, "Musicians Divide over Protesting War."
11. Benedetto and Nichols, "Rivalries Put Aside For Clinton Dedication."

her grandmother had spent hours in committee meetings at the church and noted how much nicer the new facility would be for such work.

Entertain

The *speech to entertain* makes a serious point but does it in a lighthearted manner. Traditionally, such speeches bore the title "after dinner" speeches. That name grew out of the early 1800s in England where after dinner speeches became prominent and were literally delivered following the evening meal.[12] So common were the after dinner speeches at one point in America's history that it is reported that American humorist Mark Twain delivered more than one hundred fifty such speeches during his career.[13] Today speeches to entertain may be called for at any time of the day or night, and with or without the accompanying meal.

When Dustin delivered an update on his first year of college to the hometown Rotary Club that had given him a scholarship, he used a speech to entertain. Appreciation became his serious theme, but he highlighted all of the hard work, embarrassing moments, and the week that he was sick with mono in a "thanks-a-lot" kind of satire. The speech proved to be very effective.

One of the reasons for his success was Dustin's balance between humor and his more serious point. The audience left knowing that their generosity had been appreciated but laughed heartily during the course of Dustin's presentation. That was because Dustin had used humor in a very effective and appropriate way.

Humor should be used wisely whenever it is a part of a public speaking situation. Speeches to entertain require an especially judicious use of joke telling. Humor is a complex communication phenomenon. It is unique to particular individuals as well as to particular settings. Since jokes often have more than one interpretation, what is hilarious to one individual may not strike another as the least bit funny.[14] The Family Circle cartoon that depicts one child saying to another, "I'll tell you my joke if you promise to laugh" is funny because it is so typical of real life.[15]

Jokes may also serve simply as a tension release for one individual but go too far for another who sees them as too negative, belittling, or com-

---

12. Lucas, *The Art of Public Speaking*, 479.
13. O'Hair, et al., *Speaker's Guidebook*, 402.
14. Goldstein, "Theoretical Notes on Humor," 104–12.
15. Keane, "Family Circle."

prising a put-down.[16] Successful speakers select jokes that relieve tension and only very gently tease an individual or group.

The successful celebration speaker not only determines the appropriateness of a particular piece of humor but also rehearses the joke in order to maximize impact. Timing is a critical element in the telling of a joke.[17] As a result effective pauses, which often require careful planning and diligent rehearsal, can make or break the joke.

Humor used in a speech of celebration should grow naturally out of the context of the speech topic. Jokes should be used primarily to help the speaker make the point.[18] A speech to entertain should not substitute for the routine of a standup comic or the monologue of a late night host.

The Chapter in Brief

Speeches to celebrate are sometimes called "special occasion speeches." Such speeches require a special audience analysis in order to determine the setting and audience makeup. The occasions where a speaker may be called upon to deliver such a speech include:

- Eulogizing
- Welcoming
- Introducing
- Toasting
- Nominating
- Accepting
- Dedicating
- Entertaining

Key Terms

Use the list below to test your knowledge of the vocabulary introduced in this chapter.

- speeches of celebration
- special occasion speeches
- eulogy
- welcome speech
- master of ceremonies

---

16. Smith and Power, "The Use of Disparaging Humor by Group Leaders," 279–92.
17. Palmer, *Taking Humor Seriously*, 161.
18. Meyer, "Humor as a Double-edged Sword," 310–31.

- speech of introduction
- toast
- speech of nomination
- monolithic program
- polylithic program
- speech of dedication
- one-time assembly
- on-going assembly
- speech to entertain
- speech to accept

For Review and Discussion

1. The round table discussion group could not decide if a eulogy was most like a speech to inform or a speech to persuade. Which of these two categories do you believe the speech to celebrate is most like? Defend your answer.

2. Have you seen examples of effective humor in a speech to entertain? Have you seen ineffective examples? How were the situations different?

3. Which of the eight types of speeches to celebrate do you believe would be most difficult to deliver? Why?

Proclamation Practice

Pair up with another member of your study group or class. Develop for delivery in class a two to three minute speech of celebration that builds upon role playing a scenario with that person. For example, pretend you partner has died; you give the eulogy. Or that your partner is running for governor; you make the nomination. Or imagine your partner is getting married; you give the toast.

Glossary

absolutism: System of ethics maintaining that there are absolute moral principles of right and wrong from which a decision maker may never deviate.

adaptors: Gestures that demonstrate stress or fear.

ad hominem fallacy: Fallacy of reasoning that attacks the person holding a position rather than the position itself. Also called "name-calling fallacy."

almanacs: Books of data.

analogical reasoning: Pattern of reasoning that compares two things with some similar characteristics and concludes that what is true for one will also be true for the other in every case.

appreciative listening: Listening strictly for enjoyment.

argument: Set of evidence that demonstrates a thesis statement or point.

Aristotle: Father of rhetoric, who wrote a book entitled *Rhetoric* in the fourth century B. C.

atlas: Collection of maps.

attending: Second step in the listening process.

attitude: Mental position with regard to someone or something.

audience analysis: Process by which a speaker discovers an audience's makeup and interests.

behavior: Observable actions that indicate a person's attitudes, beliefs, and values.

belief: Confidence in the existence or reality of someone or something.

biographical collections: Compilations of biographical sketches on select people.

brainstorming: Process by which a group records preliminary ideas for a speech topic. During the process no ideas are off limits, refinement occurs later.

causal reasoning: Pattern of reasoning that establishes a cause and effect relationship.

causal structure: Organizes speeches around a cause and effect format.

channel: Pathway by which a message travels from a sender to a receiver or back.

Christian testimony: Speech that indicates how a believer came to faith in Christ or how he or she has grown in that faith.

chronemics: Study of time and expectations concerning time.

chronological structure: Organizational pattern that structures a speech according to a time sequence.

circular reasoning: Assumes as a premise what is intended as a conclusion.

cognitive consistency: Individuals avoid holding two attitudes, beliefs, or values that are in opposition to one another.

cognitive dissonance: The effect of holding two attitudes, beliefs, or values that oppose one another.

commentaries: Books of explanatory notes or insights on the scripture.

communication: The act of imparting, conferring, or delivering knowledge, opinions, or facts from one individual to another.

communication apprehension: Anxiety associated with standing before a group in order to give a speech.

comparative-advantage: The organizational structure for a persuasive speech that assumes the existence of a problem and focuses on why the speaker's solution is preferable to others.

comprehending: The third step in the listening process that involves understanding the meaning of the message.

comprehensive listening: Listening while withholding judgment and listening only for understanding.

conclusion: In deductive reasoning—the necessary consequence of the major and minor premise. More generally—the end of the speech wherein the speaker makes the speech memorable and summarizes key points.

connotative meaning: Meanings of words or phrases that grow out of an individual's personal experience. Contrast *denotative meaning*.

conversational style: Speech delivery style where the speaker appears to be engaged in a one-on-one conversation with the audience.

correlation: The final step in methodical Bible study that involves blending the truths of a passage with timeless truths previously discovered.

critical listening: Listening that occurs when a listener carefully evaluates a message's strengths and weaknesses.

databases: Collections of information stored electronically.

Glossary

deductive reasoning: Pattern of reasoning where a generally accepted claim is used to reason the truth about a specific claim or claims.

definition: Statement providing the exact meaning of a word or phrase.

definitional speech: Speeches designed to explain or define terms, concepts, beliefs, theories, policies, or ideas.

demographic audience analysis: Process of discovering information such as the gender, age, socio-economic status, religion, race, or ethnicity of audience members.

demonstration speech: Speech that tells the audience how to perform a task or how something works.

denotative meaning: Meaning of a word or phrase that is found in a dictionary. Contrast *connotative meaning*.

description speech: Speech designed to paint mental pictures of persons, places, events, activities, concepts, or objects.

dictionary: Book of information about words.

edification: Process of instructing or improving the mind by means of moral or spiritual teaching.

emblems: Gestures that stand for or take the place of a word.

emotion laden words: Words that trigger an emotional response in a listener often short-circuiting the listening process.

emphatic listening: Process of listening to the concerns of another for the purpose of providing emotional support. Also called "therapeutic listening".

encyclopedias: Books that offer articles on a great variety of topics.

esteem needs: Need to feel good about self. Fourth level of needs according to Maslow's hierarchy.

ethical egoism: Ethical system that determines the morality of an act on the basis of personal self interest.

ethics: System of moral standards used to determine right and wrong.

ethos: Appeals of speaker credibility, usually from competence and experience.

environmental noise: Obstacles to message comprehension that originate in the surroundings.

eulogy: Speech to celebrate the life of a person who has died.

evaluation: Third step in methodical Bible study, involving a search for the timeless truths in the passage. Also called "application."

exegesis: Systematic study designed to discover the original intended meaning of a scripture passage.

expository lessons: Speeches to edify that set forth the meaning or expound upon a truth derived directly from a biblical text.

extemporaneous: Delivery style marked by well-prepared, conversationally delivered speeches. Contrast with *manuscript* or *memorized* style.

extrinsic credibility: Credibility that a speaker brings to the speech and that originates outside the speaking event. Contrast *intrinsic credibility*.

faith lessons: Speeches to edify that are not derived directly from the study of a particular scripture passage but do support the clear general teaching of the Bible.

fallacy: Flaw in reasoning that generates the wrong conclusion.

false impressions: True statements designed to conjure up for the audience an image that is not accurate.

fear of failure: One possible cause of communication or public speaking anxiety stemming from past performance failures projected onto current speaking events.

fear of the unknown: One possible cause of communication or public speaking anxiety resulting from inadequate preparation.

feedback: Verbal, nonverbal, intentional, or unintentional response message that results when a sender and receiver switch roles.

filler words: Unintelligible guttural sounds or meaningless words designed to fill the silence caused by natural pauses. See also *vocalized pause*.

fixed alternative questions: Questions such as true/false or agree/disagree for which there are only two possible responses.

gestures: Hand, body, or facial movements of a speaker.

global plagiarism: Using an entire speech that has been written by another.

group communication: Three or more people interacting in pursuit of a common goal.

hearing: Physiological process of obtaining sound waves through the ears.

hypothetical example: Describes an incident that did not actually occur in real life, but is typical of real life.

illustrators: Gestures that add emphasis to words but do not replace the words.

impromptu speeches: Unplanned, unrehearsed, and spontaneous speeches.

Glossary

indexes: Books that consider hundreds of periodicals and point the researcher to a particular issue that has information on the topic under review.

inductive reasoning: Pattern of reasoning that examines a series of observations in order to arrive at a general conclusion.

intellectual audience analysis: Mentally inferring what is known about an audience.

intentional plagiarism: Consciously using the words or work of another as if they were one's own.

internal previews: Appear in the body of the speech and explain what the speaker intends to convey next.

internal summaries: Statements in the body of the speech that summarize a point or points already discussed.

interpersonal communication: Communication which occurs between two people.

interpretation: Second step of methodical Bible study that raises the question "What does the passage mean?"

interview: A meeting between a speaker and a person from whom that speaker seeks information.

intrapersonal communication: Communication occurring within a single individual.

intrinsic credibility: Credibility that comes from within the speech itself as a result of the speaker's charisma or expertise. Contrast *extrinsic credibility*.

jargon: Specialized vocabulary shared by those in the same work or way of life.

journal: Periodical covering specialized material from an academic perspective.

judgment projection: Process of a speaker projecting a critical judge onto the audience and thus increasing communication anxiety.

Kantian ethics: System of ethics developed by Immanuel Kant that is based upon principles known as categorical imperatives.

logos: Logical appeals.

love needs: Third level of needs according to Maslow's hierarchy indicating that everyone has the need to love and to be loved.

major premise: Generally accepted claim that is used to begin the process of deductive reasoning.

manuscript: Word for word text of a speech.

manuscript speeches: Speeches that are read word for word from a prepared text.

Glossary

mass communication: Communication to a large or geographically disconnected audience usually occurring by means of television, radio, the World Wide Web, or print media.

master of ceremonies: Individual responsible for setting the general tone of a program and for keeping the event moving.

mean: Commonly used statistic that is calculated by adding together the values in a field of data and dividing by the total number of entries in that field.

median: Statistic representing the middle number in a list previously placed in rank order.

meeting of the minds: Agreement that exists between a sender and a receiver on the meaning of the symbols comprising a message.

memorized speeches: Speeches delivered word for word after committing them to memory during preparation.

message: Written, spoken, or unspoken symbols to which two or more people assign meaning.

minor premise: A specific point or example that fits within the major premise in the process of deductive reasoning.

mode: Number that occurs most frequently in a set of numbers.

monolithic program: Program composed of one principal speaker.

Monroe's Motivated Sequence: Persuasive speech structure developed by Alan Monroe, using five steps: attention, need, satisfaction, visualization, and action.

narrative: Story used to support a point.

New Testament ethics: System of ethics characterized by the addition of the golden rule to the Old Testament absolutes of justice, equality, holiness, and integrity.

noise: Anything that keeps a message from being understood as a sender intended.

observation: First step in methodical Bible study, involving asking, without preconceptions, what the passage is saying.

one-time assembly: Group which has come together for a unique purpose, and thus creates a unique rhetorical event.

ongoing assembly: Group such as a church, social service organization, or club that meets regularly beyond the immediate speech context.

partial truths: Leaving out some strategic facts that if known by the audience, may change their likely conclusion.

participation questions: Questions designed for audience members to answer either verbally or nonverbally.

patchwork plagiarism: Patching together large segments of speeches that have been written by others.

pathos: Emotional appeals.

peer testimony: Statements by someone, other than a professional, designed to support or prove a point.

performance visualization: Process of mentally picturing a successful speech, thus creating a positive attitude and improved performance.

persuasion: Process by which a speaker attempts to elicit a voluntary change in the attitudes, beliefs, values, or behaviors of another.

physiological needs: Lowest of the five levels of needs according to Maslow's hierarchy, including the need for air and water.

physiological noise: Obstacles to message comprehension that exist within the physical bodies of the sender or the receiver.

plagiarism: Presenting another person's words or ideas as one's own without giving proper credit.

polylithic program: Program composed of several speakers at the same event.

post-address feedback: Comments about a speech that are directed to the speaker after the speech is over.

preparation outline: Outline, written in full sentences and including a title and thesis statement that helps the speaker prepare the speech and check for all of the essential elements.

presentation outline: Outline that aids in the delivery of the speech by listing key words or phrases designed to help prevent a memory lapse.

primacy effect: The first item in a list that is heard has the longest lasting and greatest impact on the hearer.

problem/solution structure: Organizational structure for a persuasive speech that asserts first that a problem exists and then develops a proposed solution.

pro/con structure: Organizes speeches by presenting both sides of an issue in a balanced way.

professional testimony: Statement by a professional designed to support or prove a point. Also referred to as "expert testimony."

progressive spiral: Spiral that occurs when repeated positive expectations about a speech lead to a better speech.

psychological audience analysis: Seeks to discover the beliefs, values, and attitudes of an audience relative to the topic of the speech.

psychological noise: Obstacles to message comprehension that exist in the mind of either the sender or the receiver.

public speaking: Communication from one speaker to many listeners in a face to face setting.

question/answer period: A participatory technique that allows audience members to clarify their understanding of a point or points in the speech.

questionnaire: A set of written questions designed to gain data for a speech.

quotation collections: Compilations of quotations from historical and contemporary figures.

real examples: Actual, real-life incidents that support a point in a speech.

receiver: One who decodes the message from a sender in an initial attempt to understand the sender's intent.

recency effect: The last item heard in a list has the longest lasting and greatest impact.

red herring fallacy: Introduces irrelevant arguments that divert the audience's attention away from the topic at hand.

reframing the alternatives: Act of altering a topic slightly from what was assigned by the audience members or their representative. Also used in approaching an impromptu speech.

regressive spiral: In communication apprehension a regressive spiral occurs when the anticipation of anxiety repeatedly creates more anxiety.

reinforcement strategy: Strategy of persuasion designed to strengthen an audience's position when the audience and speaker are in basic agreement.

relativism: Ethical system teaching that there is no absolute moral truth and therefore no universal right and wrong.

remembering: Fourth and final step in the listening process that involves the ability to recall what has been heard.

reversal strategy: Persuasion strategy adopted by the speaker when the audience holds an initial position different than the speaker.

rhetoric: Ancient term for the study of public speaking.

rhetorical question: Questions designed for audience members to answer mentally.

roast: An event that celebrates an individual by poking good natured fun.

Glossary

safety needs: According to Maslow's hierarchy, the second level of needs, including the need for food and shelter.

scale questions: Questions designed to determine the strength of a respondent's attitude.

self-actualization needs: Need to be the best one can be and to make a lasting difference, constituting the highest level on Maslow's hierarchy of needs.

self-fulfilling prophecy: Process of anticipating certain outcomes and then behaving as if those outcomes already exist, thus creating as a reality what was anticipated.

sender: One, who, through the process of encoding, places thoughts, ideas, or emotions into a form that has the potential to be understood by a receiver.

signposts: Words or statements that point the way where a speaker plans to go in a speech.

situational audience analysis: Considers the size of the audience and the physical setting where the speech will take place.

slang: Language outside conventional or standard usage, usually with a new or extended meaning.

slippery slope fallacy: Assumes that going the first step will inevitably lead to ultimate disaster.

spatial structure: Organizes a speech by creating a mental picture based on geographic or directional characteristics.

special occasion speeches: Speeches designed to celebrate a specific event or person. See also *speech to celebrate*.

speech of acceptance: Celebration speech designed to acknowledge an honor or award.

speech of dedication: Celebration speech that honors a person by associating their name with a permanent fixture such as a building, room, monument, or plaque.

speech of introduction: Speech in which the speaker introduces another.

speech of nomination: Speech placing the name of an individual before a group for elected office or to receive an honor or award.

speech speed: Rate at which a speaker talks, averaging in America one hundred twenty to one hundred fifty words per minute.

speech to celebrate: Speeches designed to celebrate a specific event or person. See also *special-occasion speeches*.

speech to entertain: Celebration speech making a serious point in a lighthearted manner.

speech to inform: Speech about objects, people, events, processes, concepts, or issues designed to enhance an audience member's knowledge or understanding.

speech topic: Broad subject matter covered by speech.

speech type: Purpose of a speech including inform, persuade, edify, or celebrate.

statement of fact: Statements concerning what is or is not true.

statement of policy: Statements claiming that a certain course of action should or should not be taken.

statement of value: Statements affirming something as good or bad, moral or immoral, right or wrong.

statistics: Numerical reports of research findings.

stereotyping: Applying a particular characteristic to an entire people group.

thesis statement: One sentence statement of what the speaker hopes to accomplish in the speech.

thought speed: Rate at which an audience member thinks, typically four hundred to eight hundred words per minute.

toast: Celebration speech offering a brief tribute in honor of an individual or group.

topical structure: Speech structure accomplished by dividing topics into component sub-topics. Often used for speeches to inform.

transitions: Words, phrases, or sentences in a speech acting as bridges by linking one part of the speech to the next.

unintentional plagiarism: Unconsciously using the words of another in a speech as a result of sloppy research or careless notetaking.

utilitarianism: Ethical system asserting that the decision producing the most good or the least harm for the most people is the ethical choice.

value: Indicator of the relative worth, usefulness, or general importance of something.

verbal citation: Giving credit in a speech by providing enough information so that an audience member can find the source if they so desire.

vocalized pause: Unintelligible guttural sounds or meaningless word designed to fill the silence caused by natural pauses. See also *filler words*.

welcome speech: Celebration speech designed to greet an individual or group.

yearbook: Book that summarizes the activities of the past year or offers certain kinds of helps for the current year.

Bibliography

Abraham, Priya. "Let My People Go." *World* (February 24, 2007) 17–19.
Ackerman, Dianne. *Great Souls: Six Who Changed The Century.* Nashville: Word, 1998.
Alessandra, Tony. *Charisma: Seven Keys To Developing The Magnetism That Leads To Success.* New York: Warner, 2000.
Allen, Ron J. *Preaching: An Essential Guide.* Nashville: Abingdon, 2002.
Axtell, Roger E. *Do's and Taboos of Public Speaking: How to Get Those Butterflies Flying In Formation.* New York: Wiley, 1992.
Ayres, Joe, and Tim Hopf. *Coping With Speech Anxiety.* Norwood, NJ: Ablex, 1993.
Baddeley, Alan D. *Your Memory: A User's Guide.* Richmond Hill, Ontario: Firefly Books, 2004.
Banach, William J. "Are You Too Busy to Think?" *Vital Speeches of the Day* 57, no.11 (1991): 351–53.
Barker, Larry, et al. "An Investigation of Proportional Time Spent in Various Communication Activities by College Students." *Journal of Applied Communication Research* 8 (1981): 101–109.
Barnette, James. "I Stand Here Testifying: Applying Paul's Use of Autobiography to Our Preaching." *Preaching* 20, no. 3 (2004): 22–26.
Bates, Jane. "Unaccustomed as I Am . . . " *Nursing Standard* 19, no. 14 (2004): 25–27.
Beebe, Steven A., et al. *Communication: Principles for a Lifetime.* Boston: Allyn and Bacon, 2001.
Benedetto, Richard, and Bill Nichols. "Rivalries Put Aside For Clinton Dedication." *USA Today*, November 19, 2004, sec. A.
Bostrom, Robert R., and Carol L. Bryant. "Factors in the Retention of Information Presented Orally: The Role of Short-term Listening." *Western Journal of Speech Communication* 44 (1980): 137–45.
Bragg, Rick. *I Am A Soldier, Too: The Jessica Lynch Story.* New York: Alfred A Knopf, 2003.
Callison, Daniel, and Annette Lamb. "Audience Analysis." *School Library Media Activities Monthly* 21, no.1 (2004): 34–40.
Canfield, Jack. *The Success Principles: How to Get From Where You Are To Where You Want To Be.* New York: Harper Collins, 2005.
Carey, Bryccan. "William Wilberforce (1759–1833)." http://www.brycchancarey.com/abolition/ wilberforce.htm (accessed February 17, 2007).
Carter, Rosalyn. *The First Lady from Plains.* New York: Houghton Mifflin, 1984.
Chua-Evans, Howard, and Elizabeth Gleick. "Making the Case." *Time*, October 16, 1995, 48–61.
Coakley, Carolyn, and Andrew Wolvin. "Listening in the Educational Environment." In *Listening in Everyday Life: A Personal and Professional Approach,* 2nd ed. edited by Michael Purdy and Deborah Borisoff, 179–212, Lanham, MD: University Press, 1997.
Colwell, Robert P. "Brainstorming: Influence and Icebergs." *Computer* 37, no. 4 (2004): 9–13.

Bibliography

Cowherd, Kevin. "Speaking in Public no Scarier Than Flying." *Ft. Wayne Journal Gazette*, December 23, 1989, sec. B.

Curtis, Dan B., et al. "National Preferences in Business and Communication Education." *Communication Education* 38, no. 1 (1989): 6–14.

Darrow, Rob. "Using the Big 6 to Write a Thesis Statement for High School English and History Students." *Library Media Connection* 23, no. 5 (2005): 36.

DeVito, Joseph A. *The Elements of Public Speaking*. 7th ed. New York: Longman, 2000.

Ekman, Paul, and Wallace V. Friesen. "The Repertoire of Nonverbal Behavior: Categories, Origins, Usage, and Coding." *Semiotica* 1, no. 1 (1969): 49–98.

Engleberg, Isa N. *The Principles of Public Presentation*. New York: Harper Collins, 1994.

Fee, Gordon D. and Douglas K. Stuart. *How to Read the Bible for All It's Worth*. Grand Rapids: Zondervan, 2003.

Festinger, Leon. *A Theory of Cognitive Dissonance*. Stanford, CA: Stanford University Press, 1962.

Finkel, Ed. "Sticky Fingers on the Information Superhighway." *Community College Week* 17, no. 15 (2005): 6–9.

Fletcher, Joseph F. *Situation Ethics: The New Morality*. Philadelphia: Westminster, 1966.

Frank, S. "I'll Show You My Underwear (Or How to Tackle the Dreaded Thesis Statement)." *Writing* 27, no. 4 (2005): 14–18.

Frymier, Ann Bainbridge, and Gary M. Shulman. "What's in it for me? Increasing Content Relevance to Enhance Students' Motivation." *Communication Education* 44 (1995): 40–50.

Gardner, Howard. *Changing Minds: The Art and Science of Changing Our Own and Other People's Minds*. Boston: Harvard Business School, 2004.

Gelles-Cole, Sandi. Ed. *Letitia Baldridge's Complete Guide to Executive Manners*. New York: Rawson Associates, 1985.

Gibson, Scott M. "Biblical Preaching in An Anti-authority Age." In *Preaching to a Shifting Culture: 12 Perspectives on Communicating That Counts,* edited by Scott M. Gibson, 215–227, Grand Rapids: Baker, 2004.

Goldstein, Jeffrey H. "Theoretical Notes on Humor." *Journal of Communication* 26 (1976): 104–12.

Golob, Edward J., and Arnold Starr. "Serial Position Effects in Auditory Event: Related Potentials During Working Memory Retrieval." *Journal of Cognitive Neuroscience* 16, no. 1 (2004): 40–53.

Gorham, Joan and Stanley H. Cohen. "Fashion in the Classroom III: Effects of Instructor Attire and Immediacy in Natural Classroom Instruction." *Communication Quarterly* 47, no. 3 (1999): 281–99.

Graham, Billy. *Storm Warnings*. Dallas: Word, 1992.

Gronbeck, Bruce E., et al. *Principles and Types of Speech Communication*. 14th ed. New York: Longman, 2001.

Gruner, Charles R. "Advice to the Beginning Speaker on Using Humor: What the Research Tells Us." *Communication Education* 34 (1985): 142–47.

Halone, Kelby K., et al. "Toward the Establishment of General Dimensions Underlying the Listening Process." *International Journal of Listening* 12 (1988): 12–28.

Hamilton, Lee. "A Responsibility for Civility." *State Legislatures* 31, no. 1 (2005): 19.

Heider, Fritz. *Psychology of Interpersonal Relations*. New York: Wiley and Sons, 1958.

Hock, Randolph. *The Extreme Searchers Guide To Web Search Engines: A Handbook for the Serious Researcher,* 2nd ed., Medford, NJ: Information Today, 2001.

Hosmer, LaRue Tone. *The Ethics of Management* 3rd ed. Chicago: Irwin, 1996.

Bibliography

Hubbard, Burt, and Jerd Smith. "Offender System Shines: Youth Rehab Program Makes Great Strides Despite Big Obstacles." *Rocky Mountain News*, January 4, 2005, sec. 5.

Irvine, Martha. "Dress Codes Get Back To Business: Many Employers, Schools Tightening Up Apparel Rules." *Marion-Chronicle Tribune*, September 9, 2004, sec. A.

Jacobs, A. J. "How to Relax in Public." *Esquire* 142, no. 2 (2004): 38.

Jaffe, Clella. *Public Speaking: Concepts and Skills for a Diverse Society.* 4th ed. Belmont, CA: Wadsworth/Thomson, 2004.

Jenkins, Roy., *Churchill: A Biography.* New York: Farrar, Straus, and Giroux, 2001.

Johnson, John R. and Nancy Szczupakiewicz. "The Public Speaking Course: Is It Preparing Students With Work-Related Public Speaking Skills?" *Communication Education* 36 (1987): 131–37.

Johnson, Scott D., and Christopher F. Roelke. "Secondary Teachers' and Undergraduate Education Faculty Members' Perceptions of Teaching-Effectiveness Criteria: A national Survey." *Communication Education* 48 no. 1 (1999) 127–38.

Jones, Bob. "Red ink, purple ink." *World*, February 12, 2005, 20–21.

Kant, Immanuel. *Groundwork of the Metaphysics of Morals.* Translated by H. J. Paton. New York: Harper and Row, 1964.

Karr, Albert R. "A Special News Report About Life on the Job—And Trends Taking Shape There." *The Wall Street Journal*, December 29, 1998, sec. A.

Keane, Bil. "Family Circle." *Marion Chronicle-Tribune*, January 31, 2007, sec. B.

Kenworthy, Tom. "Rally at Wellstone Memorial Cited in GOP Victory in Minnesota." *USA Today,* November 7, 2002, sec. A.

Kissell, Joe. "The Toast: Here's to the Ritual of Raised Glasses." *Interesting Thing of the Day*, April 13, 2005, http://itold.com/articles/518/the-toast.

Levy, Steven. "The World According to Google." *Newsweek*, December 16, 2002, 46–51.

Litfin, Duane. *Public Speaking: A Handbook for Christians.* 2nd ed. Grand Rapids, MI: Baker, 1992.

Lucas, Stephen E. *The Art of Public Speaking,* 9th ed. New York: McGraw Hill, 2007.

Lundsteen, Sara W. "Metacognitive Listening." In *Perspectives on* Listening, edited by A.D. Wolvin and C. G. Coakley, 106–23, Norwood, NJ: Ablex, 1993.

McCroskey, James C. *An Introduction to Rhetorical Communication.* 9th ed. Boston, MA: Allyn and Bacon, 2006.

McDill, Wayne V. *The Moment of Truth.* Nashville: Broadman and Holman, 1999.

McKenna, Barbara J., and John J. McKenna. "Selecting Topics for Research Writing Projects." *English Journal* 89, no. 6 (2000): 53–59.

Maes, Jeanne D., et al. "A Managerial Perspective: Oral Communication Competency is Most Important for Business Students in the Workplace," *Journal of Business Communication,* 34 no. 1 (1997): 67–80.

Maher, Kris. "Career Journal: The Jungle." *The Wall Street Journal*, February 4, 2003, sec. B.

Mansfield, Brian. "The Chicks Ruffle Some Feathers." *USA Today*, March 19, 2003, sec. D.

Maslow, Abraham. "A Theory of Human Motivation." *Psychological Review* 50 (1970): 370–96.

Maxwell, John C. *There's No Such Thing as Business Ethics.* New York: Time Warner, 2003.

Meyer, John C. "Humor as a Double-edged Sword: Four Functions of Humor in Communication." *Communication Theory* (2000): 310–31.

Miller, Zell. *A National Party No More: The Conscience of a Conservative Democrat.* Atlanta: Stroud and Hall, 2003.

Mulac, Anthony, and A. R. Sherman. "Behavioral Assessment of Speech Anxiety." *Quarterly Journal of Speech* 60 (1974): 134–43.

Bibliography

Murphree, Jon Tal. *Responsible Evangelism: Relating Theory to Practice.* Toccoa Falls, GA: Toccoa Falls College, 1994.
Neff, Blake J. *A Pastor's Guide to Interpersonal Communication: The Other Six Days.* Binghamton, NY: Haworth, 2006.
Newcomb, Theodore M. *The Acquaintance Process.* New York: Holt, Rinehart, and Winston, 1961.
Nichols, Michael P. *The Lost Art of Listening.* New York: Guilford, 1995.
Nijstad, Bernard A. et al. "Production Blocking and Idea Generation: Does Blocking Interfere with Cognitive Processes?" *Journal of Experimental Social Psychology* 39, no. 6 (2003): 531–49.
Noonan, Peggy. *When Character Was King: A Story of Ronald Reagan.* New York: Viking, 2001.
Oberauer, Klaus. "Understanding Serial Position Curves in Short-term Recognition and Recall." *Journal of Memory and Language* 49, no. 4 (2003): 469–84.
O'Hair, Dan, et al. *Speaker's Guidebook: Text and Reference.* Bedford: St Martins, 2007.
O'Hair, Dan and Rob Stewart. *Public Speaking: Challenges and Choices.* Boston: Bedford/St. Martin's, 1999.
Olford, Stephen F. *Anointed Expository Preaching.* Nashville: Broadman and Holman, 1998.
Osgood, Charles E. and P. H. Tannenbaum. "The Principle of Congruity in the Prediction of Attitude Change." *Psychological Review* 62, no. 1 (1955): 42–55.
Palmer, Jerry. *Taking Humor Seriously.* London: Routledge, 1994.
Post, Peggy. *Emily Post's Wedding Etiquette.* 4th ed. New York: Harper Collins, 2001.
Rae, Scott B. *Moral Choices,* 2nd ed. Grand Rapids: Zondervan, 2000.
Richmond, Virginia P. and James C. McCroskey. *Nonverbal Behavior in Interpersonal Relations.* 4th ed. Boston: Allyn and Bacon, 2000.
Roach, Carol A. and Nancy J. Wyatt. "Listening and the Rhetorical Process." In *Bridges Not Walls: A Book About Interpersonal Communication,* 5th ed., edited by John Stewart, 171–76. New York: McGraw Hill, 1995.
_____. *Successful Listening.* New York: Harper and Row, 1988.
Roberts, Caroline. "Plagiarism." *Times Educational Supplement*, November 26, 2004, 11.
Robinson, Haddon W. "The Relevance of Expository Preaching." In *Preaching To a Shifting Culture: 12 Perspectives on Communication That Counts,* edited by Scott M. Gibson, 79–93. Grand Rapids: Baker, 2004.
Rokeach, Milton. *The Nature of Human Values.* New York: Free Press, 1973.
Schacter, Daniel L. *The Seven Sins Of Memory: How The Mind Forgets and Remembers.* Boston: Houghton Mifflin, 2002.
Schultze, Quentin. *An Essential Guide to Public Speaking.* Grand Rapids: Baker, 2006.
Seiler, Kerstin H., and Johannes Engelkamp. "The Role of Item-specific Information for the Serial Position Curve in Free Recall." *Journal of Experimental Psychology/Learning, Memory and Cognition* 29, no. 5 (2003): 954–65.
Seinfeld, Jerry. *Sein Language.* New York: Bantom, 1993.
Sellnow, Deanna D. *Confident Public Speaking.* 2nd ed. Belmont, CA: Thomson Wadsworth, 2005.
Serpick, Evan. "Musicians Divide Over Protesting the War." *USA Today*, March 6, 2003, sec. D.
Smith, Christie McGuffie, and Larry Power. "The Use of Disparaging Humor by Group Leaders." *Southern Speech Communication Journal* 53 (1988): 279–92.
Snedeker, Mike. "The Great Cats." Speech to inform, Introduction to Communication, Indiana Wesleyan University, Marion, IN, Spring, 2005.

Bibliography

Sprague, Jo and Douglas Stuart. *The Speaker's Handbook* 6th ed. Belmont, CA: Wadsworth/Thomson, 2003.

Steil, Lyman K., et al. *Effective Listening: Key To Your Success*. Reading MA: Addison-Wesley, 1983.

Stinson, L. Marilyn, and Jo Ann Asquith. "Excellent Communication Skills Are an Essential Part of Being an Accountant." *Journal of Technical Writing and Communication* 27, no. 4 (1997): 385–90.

Storey, A. "Communication Fears, Simple Fixes." *Health* 18, no. 8 (2004): 104–06.

Stott, John R. *Between Two Worlds*. Grand Rapids: Wm B. Eerdmans, 1982.

Stowers, Robert H., and G. Thomas White. "Connecting Accounting and Communication: A Survey of Public Accounting Firms." *Communication Quarterly* 62 (1999): 23–31.

Temple, L. E., and K. R. Loewen. "Perceptions of Power: First Impressions of a Woman Wearing a Jacket." *Perceptual and Motor Skills* 76 (1993): 339–48.

Thourlby William. *You Are What You Wear*. New York: Forbes/Wittenburg and Brown, 2001.

Tileston, Donna Walker. *What Every Teacher Should Know About Learning, Memory, and the Brain*. Thousand Oaks, CA: Corwin, 2004.

Titsworth, B. Scott. "The Effects of Teacher Immediacy Use of Organizational Lectures Cues, and Students' Notetaking on Cognitive Learning." *Communication Education* 50 (2001): 283–97.

Traina, Robert A. *Methodical Bible Study*. Grand Rapid: Zondervan, 1980.

Trank, Douglas M., and P. Lewis. "The Introductory Communication Course: Results of a National Survey." *Basic Communication Course Annual* 3 (1991): 106–22.

Van Wyk, Robert N. *An Introduction to Ethics*. New York: St. Martins, 1990.

Verderber, Rudolph F., and Kathleen S. Verderber. *The Challenge of Effective Speaking*. 13th ed. Belmont, CA: Thomson/Wadsworth, 2006.

Wallechinsky, David, et al. *The Book of Lists*. New York: Bantam, 1977.

Wangerin, Walter Jr. (2004). "Making Disciples by Sacred Story." *Christianity Today*, February, 2004, 66–69.

Wanzer, Melissa Bekelja, and Ann Bainbridge Frymier. "The Relationship between Student Perceptions of Instructor Humor and Students' Reports of Learning." *Communication Education* 48 (1999): 48–62.

Ward, Richard F. *Speaking of the Holy*. St. Louis: Chalice, 2001.

Wilder, Lilyan. *7 Steps to Fearless Speaking*. New York: Wiley, 1999.

Wilson, Craig. "11 Great Places to Hear (or Tell) a Great Story." *USA Today*, September 28, 2001, sec. D.

World. "What are the odds?", April 16, 2005, 11.

Wolvin, Andrew D. and Diana Corley. "The Technical Speech Communication Course: A View From the Field." *Association for Communication Administration Bulletin* 49 (1984): 83–91.

Wolvin, Andrew, and Carolyn Gwynn Coakley. "A Survey of the Status of Listening Training in Some Fortune 500 Corporations." *Communication Education* 40 (1991): 152–64.

_____. *Listening*. 5th ed. Dubuque, IA: Brown, 1995.

Wyllie, James. "Oral Communication: Survey and Suggestions." *ABCA Bulletin* (1980): 15.

Zekeri, Andrew A. "College Curriculum Competencies and Skills Former Students Found Essential to Their Careers." *College Student Journal* 38, no. 3 (2004): 412–23.

www.ingramcontent.com/pod-product-compliance
Lightning Source LLC
Chambersburg PA
CBHW060606230426
43670CB00011B/1996